Threatened with $\mathcal{R}$esurrection

Self-Preservation and Christ's Way of Peace

Jim S. Amstutz

Herald
Press

Scottdale, Pennsylvania
Waterloo, Ontario

Library of Congress Cataloging-in-Publication Data
Amstutz, Jim S., 1954-
Threatened with resurrection : self-preservation and Christ's way
of peace / Jim S. Amstutz
  p. cm.
Includes bibliographical references and index.
ISBN 0-8361-9192-7 (alk. paper)
1. Peace—Religious aspects—Mennonites. 2. Self-preservation—
  Religious aspects—Mennonites. 3. Mennonites—Doctrines. I. Title.
BX8128.P4 A56 2002
230'.97—dc21
                                                        2001004479

The paper used in this publication is recycled and meets the minimum require-
ments of American National Standard for Information Sciences—Permanence
of Paper for Printed Library Materials, ANSI Z39.48-1984.

Unless otherwise noted, Scripture is used by permission, with all rights
reserved, from the *New Revised Standard Version Bible*, copyright 1989 by the
Division of Christian Education of the National Council of the Churches of
Christ in the USA.

Excerpt on page seven is from Julia Esquivel, *Threatened with Resurrection:
Prayers and Poems from an Exiled Guatemalan*, 2d ed. (Elgin, Ill.: Brethren
Press, 1994).

THREATENED WITH RESURRECTION
Copyright © 2002 by Herald Press, Scottdale, Pa. 15683
  Published simultaneously in Canada by Herald Press,
  Waterloo, Ont. N2L 6H7. All rights reserved
Library of Congress Catalog Card Number: 2001004479
International Standard Book Number: 0-8361-9192-7
Printed in the United States of America
Book and cover design by Gwen M. Stamm

10 09 08 07 06 05 04 03 02 01 10 9 8 7 6 5 4 3 2 1

To order or request information, please call 1-800-759-4447
(individuals); 1-800-245-7894 (trade). Website: www.mph.org

In a godlessly violent world, self-preservation appears self-evident. It is not easy to make sense of Christian pacifism. But in stunningly brief compass, and in disarmingly simple and straightforward prose, Jim Amstutz here shows how the Christian refusal to accept the world as godless, in the light of the peace-pregnant life of Jesus and God's kingdom, inevitably unfolds into a life of active nonviolence. At the popular level, this book is the single best case for why Christians are (or should be) pacifists, and how we might really live without killing our enemies.
—*Rodney Clapp, author and publisher, Brazos Press*

What a gift to read this book! Jim writes with pastoral sensitivity without sacrificing responsible treatment of the scriptures. I am very pleased to have a new, readable book to put in the hands of people (including pastors) for whom the language and teaching of nonresistance are unfamiliar. If we are going to be a missional church we need books like this for discipling new believers. The thirteen chapters will make an excellent alternate series for a Sunday school class. Small groups will find it provocative. Rooting the idea of peacemaking and pacifism in the resurrection of Jesus provides a powerful and fresh theological foundation for this important theme.
—*James M. Lapp, conference pastor,*
  Franconia Mennonite Conference

With clear biblical grounding, and the strength of personal experience, Jim Amstutz issues a challenging and compelling call for Christians to abandon the world's way of self-preservation and follow Jesus' way of nonviolence and peace.
—*Joyce Hollyday, author of* Then Shall Your Light Shine

Stimulating reading! Jim Amstutz takes the resurrection, the crowning event in Christian theology, and makes it relevant to how we relate to our neighbors and our enemies.
—*Titus Peachey, director of peace education,*
  Mennonite Central Committee U.S.

*To Lorraine, my best friend and peacemaker
in her own right; and my children, Sol, Jordan,
and Leah. I love you all so very much.*

To dream awake,

to keep watch asleep,

to live while dying,

and to know ourselves already

resurrected!

—Julia Esquivel, "They Have Threatened
Us with Resurrection"

Contents

Preface

This book was birthed in the context of congregational life and it is to that setting I offer it for study and conversation. I have been preaching and teaching Christ's way of peace since 1980 when I was a novice member of the Mennonite Central Committee (MCC) U.S. Peace Section. Draft registration had just been reinstated for eighteen-year-old males and it was my task to keep Mennonite pastors and churches trained and informed should military conscription and alternative service become reality once again. I quickly found myself an apologist for the Anabaptist peace position, something all of us are called upon to become when we say Yes to Jesus in that tradition. Like all issues of faith and life, each generation of Christians must claim for themselves the conviction to follow Christ in life. The way of peace Jesus taught may be considered one of the most difficult teachings to embrace, but once embraced can bring us new freedom and fresh courage.

I write as a pastor and as a Mennonite to a Christian audience. I make the assumption that we are people of the Word and that a serious study of the Scriptures not only guides us but transforms us. I assume that following Christ in life means we are ready to ask the hard questions of how to apply what Jesus said and how he lived to our lives. And I assume that what I have written will inform our cultural as well as theological imaginations. I have attempted to write in an accessible, teaching-preaching style that may disappoint some of my academic friends. My goal (and gift?) is to make weighty matters understandable and relevant to the broadest possible readership while at the same time doing careful research and preparation. Endnotes are included for those who want to go deeper.

My prayer is that the life, death, and resurrection of Jesus Christ becomes real in new and provocative ways to the reader, preferably in a group context. Classes and study groups might find it beneficial to read each chapter out loud together. I don't presume to have all the answers or to have even raised all of the right questions. But I do believe the stumbling block of self-preservation cuts to the heart of how we approach Christ's way of peace in our time.

And the peace of God, which surpasses all understanding, will guard your hearts and your minds in Christ Jesus (Phil. 4:7).

* * *

I first want to thank Phil Bergey, Bill Brunk, and Elaine Moyer for giving me the nod to develop a paper on Christ's way of peace for the Franconia Conference consultation, February 6, 1999, which led to the idea for this book. Salford Mennonite and later Swamp Mennonite invited me to do some hands-on teaching and preaching for which I am grateful.

Michael A. King, editor of Pandora Press was kind enough to not only affirm the potential of taking this to the next level but introduced me to S. David Garber of Herald Press.

Many thanks to John Stoner, my mentor and spiritual friend for twenty years. My men's group of Anabaptist pastors: Tim Weaver, Joe Hyatt, and Jeff Rill who kept me grounded and helped proofread. To Bonnie Klassen, Byron Guzman, Mike Schaadt, and the West Swamp High School Youth Class for pointing out inconsistencies and thinking out loud with me. To Pastor David Ellis, UCC pastor and former military chaplain, who made me own up to and articulate my assumptions. And to my wife and most coveted critic, Lorraine Stutzman Amstutz, for giving the manuscript the relevancy test.

To my parents, Fred and Mary Amstutz, for their lifelong support and encouragement, and to my brothers Dan, Steve, and Pete for teaching me how to fight fair and remember my roots. To K-Group, BASIC, House Church, DINKS and FAMWIE who nurtured my sense of Christian community.

Finally, to West Swamp Mennonite Church who shaped my pastoral identity, practiced Agreeing and Disagreeing in Love, and provided the pulpit, classroom, and much of the inspiration to write this book.

1
The Cross as Foolishness

"Survival is the ultimate ideology." [1]

Key Text *1 Corinthians 1:18*
> For the message about the cross is foolishness to those who are perishing, but to us who are being saved it is the power of God.

Stemming the tide. In his biography of Harold S. Bender, considered by many to be the foremost Mennonite leader during the mid-20th century, Albert N. Keim tells of the erosion of belief and practice among Mennonites during World War II. Instead of taking the expected conscientious objector position and performing Civilian Public Service (CPS), large numbers of Mennonite young men were accepting drafted or enlisted positions in the military. Keim writes:

> The apparent weakness of Mennonite convictions for nonresistance seemed to offer confirmation that Mennonites were drifting into conformity with the national ethos. Something had to be done to stem the tide and remedy the situation. [2]

The response was to make participation in the military a test of church membership, a practice still in place in many Mennonite churches today. The genesis of this book came, in fact, out of a discussion on church membership and military involvement that I had in an area conference. How do we respond to fellow or potential church members whose job requires them to carry a weapon? How do we stem the tide of cultural assimilation with the assumption that defending ourselves or our loved ones with lethal violence is "normal," even expected of us?

Self-preservation at all costs. Self-preservation is indeed woven into the very fabric of our North American culture. From national defense policies to the constitutional right to bear arms to car alarms and home security systems, society assumes that everyone has the right, even the *obligation* to protect themselves, and by extension their loved ones. Preserving the self seems natural and, at a basic level, that is how living things are created. We seek shelter, food, and clothing to protect our survival. But beyond those basic and essential needs is our response to forces that could harm or kill us. We take common sense measures like strapping on a seatbelt when we drive or wearing protective clothing in a snowstorm. We lock our doors at night and install security lights around our homes and businesses. But what about the "ultimate ideology" of survival? What about self-preservation at all costs? Are people of faith justified in taking a life to save a life? What should responsible and faithful Christians do in the face of lethal violence? Do the Bible and Jesus give us any guidance for survival in the real world when our very lives are threatened?

The highest good? If self-preservation is the highest moral good, as society assumes, and blessed by God, as most Christian traditions assume, then why didn't Jesus find a way out of going to the cross? Why didn't God or the disciples intervene to prevent the innocent execution of Jesus? Why didn't Jesus just slip away from Jerusalem (flight) or mount an armed rebellion (fight) when the cross loomed large? The fact that he did neither is what this book is about.

The cross as foolishness. Each year I offer a membership seminar for those new to our church or the Mennonite faith. We meet during the Sunday school hour for three months. I always include at least one session on the biblical way of peace and one year I learned an important lesson. We wrestled with the hard sayings of Jesus about peace and the "What would you do. . . ?"[3] questions that inevitably come up. What was different about this particular discussion was the timing. Taking this on during the first month of the class, as opposed to later in the quarter, proved to be difficult at best, and a stumbling block for several potential members. Three decided not to join, primarily because of this difficult teaching. Eventually I realized that new believers and seekers have a hard time seeing past the finality of the cross. Challenging the assumption of self-preservation is foolish to those who only see death without resurrection.

Challenging the pervasive assumption of self-preservation makes no sense unless we approach it from a faith perspective. Without resurrection hope to guide us, and the Holy Spirit to empower us, embracing this difficult yet essential understanding of faith is indeed foolish. We need to keep this in mind if we are going to allow our faith to take us somewhere most of us do not ever want to go.

Fools for Christ. You've seen the omnipresent signs at sporting events. Someone in the stands holds up a brightly painted sign with John 3:16 on it. "Fools for Christ" might be a generous way to describe these poster-board evangelists. Does holding up the sign lead anyone to faith? Perhaps. But more often than not, most of us let the sign simply become part of the background scenery, part of the crowd noise at a sporting event. The sign loses its significance because it no longer shocks or confronts our sensibilities. The same thing can be said about the cross. We've domesticated the cross by making it a familiar symbol in our culture. We forget that the cross in Jesus' day represented the death penalty. Do you know anyone who wears a gold-plated electric chair or syringe around his or her neck on Sunday morning?

For God so loved. Let's look at John 3:16 and add verse 17:

> For God so loved the world that he gave his only Son, so that everyone who believes in him may not perish but may have eternal life. Indeed, God did not send the Son into the world to con-

demn the world, but in order that the world might be saved
through him.

God approaches the world (Greek *cosmos*) in love with the
purpose of salvation. This big picture view helps us understand the way of God and the cross. The response of Jesus to
lethal violence gives us a clear understanding of how God
wants to save the world. What Jesus taught about enemies
and suffering and sacrifice is consistent with and supports his
actions when he was faced with execution. The keystone to
this approach is the resurrection. Without the resurrection,
those who put Jesus to death win. The forces of evil prevail.
Injustice and "might makes right" are vindicated. But on the
third day Jesus rose from the dead. Not only does that fact
save us from sin and eternal death at the end of our life, it also
sets the stage for overcoming evil with good while we're alive,
and when we are face-to-face with death. So those times that
we are threatened with death, we are really threatened with
resurrection.[4]

Who's fooling whom? Paul told the church in Corinth that the
cross of Christ was foolishness to those who are perishing but
to those who believe it is the power of God. If we confess that
God is the most powerful force in the universe and that Jesus
as God's Son had that power at his disposal then the *self-lim-
itation* of that power is a lesson we dare not miss. God could
force us to go the way of obedience, but out of love and respect for our free will we are not forced. Similarly, God could
have wiped out any opposition to Jesus or the malevolent
forces at work that put Jesus to death. Instead, God chose not
to fight fire with fire or to meet deadly force with greater force.
The power of God at work in Jesus was the power of holy
love, the power of holy surrender, the power of holy resurrection. Romans 5:10 says, "For if, when we were *God's enemies*,
we were reconciled to him through the death of his Son . . ."
(NIV, emphasis mine). Consistent with God's loving character,

holy love is employed to reconcile those alienated from God because of sin. But God doesn't clobber us into submission. The holy surrender of Jesus is one that, on the surface, seems like utter defeat. The two disciples on the road to Emmaus (Luke 24:13f.) were leaving the Holy City because their leader had been killed. They told the stranger traveling with them "But we had hoped that he was the one to redeem Israel" (v. 21). In their minds the hope for redemption (in this case for Israel) died with Jesus on the cross. His surrender meant the end of the movement. When they recognized him in the breaking of the bread (symbolic of his own brokenness) they immediately got up and headed back into the city in spite of the inherent dangers of traveling at night (v. 33). What turned them around was the power of holy resurrection. It was that new reality that empowered the disciples to boldly proclaim the gospel message, even in the face of severe persecution. God's way became the way of the early church and becomes our way when we embrace the power of resurrection hope.

When we say YES to Jesus and confess him as Lord and Savior we also claim his resurrection hope. That by definition influences how we approach all of life, and perhaps most important, how we approach our death. The fear of death can immobilize us the way it did the disciples before they discovered the empty tomb. But resurrection hope can empower us to overcome that fear and guide us in our discernment of faithful discipleship. Picking up our cross to follow Jesus may mean a direct confrontation with the principalities and powers that put Jesus on the cross he was carrying. On the other hand, following Christ in death also means following Christ into new life, and that makes all the difference.

The chapters that follow will address some of the "what ifs" and "yes, buts" that are likely running through your mind. Our faith calls us to challenge the assumption of choosing self-preservation at all costs and instead claim the power of God as we follow Christ in life and death and resurrection.

Questions for Discussion

1. What evidence do you observe that the doctrine of self-preservation permeates our culture?
2. Do you agree with the dichotomy between basic survival and self-preservation at all costs? Is this an artificial distinction or one that Christians need to understand and teach?
3. How have we domesticated the cross and/or the gospel?
4. What is a new thought or idea that jumped out at you today? Do you feel challenged, affirmed, confused?
5. How does the resurrection influence how we make decisions as people of faith? Think of a specific example or application.
6. What is God trying to say to you today? To your class or small group? To your church?

2
Cross Purposes

The original Christians, in short, were about creating and sustaining a unique culture—a way of life that would shape character in the image of their God. And they were determined to be a culture, a quite public and political culture, even if it killed them and their children.

—Rodney A. Clapp[1]

Key Text *Matthew 16:21-25*
From that time on, Jesus began to show his disciples that he must go to Jerusalem and undergo great suffering at the hands of the elders and chief priests and scribes, and be killed, and on the third day be raised. And Peter took him aside and began to rebuke him, saying, "God forbid it, Lord! This must never happen to you." But he turned and said to Peter, "Get behind me, Satan! You are a stumbling block to me; for you are setting your mind not on divine things but on human things." Then Jesus told his disciples, "If any want to become my followers, let them deny themselves and take up their cross and follow me. For those who want to save their life will lose it, and those who lose their life for my sake will find it.

My mother's side of the family is Russian Mennonite. My grandparents, Abram and Anna Wiebe Schmidt, were among the three hundred or so families who fled East to Harbin, China. There, while waiting for sponsorship from North American Mennonites, my aunt was born. My four uncles were young boys, with John still in diapers. After a year of waiting they found their way to California and eventually to land owned by Bluffton College in Ohio. My mother was born there. My grandfather succumbed to a bleeding ulcer when my mother was only four. Times were tough for these German-speaking Russian Mennonites living in the Swiss Mennonite enclave of Bluffton and Pandora.[2]

Fitting in was important. As World War II approached, my uncles followed the path of most of their peers—they enlisted in the armed forces. Would they have chosen differently had their father survived? We will never know. Refugees often prove their loyalty to their host country by joining the military in times of war. My uncles were no exception and I may have chosen the same path had I been in their shoes. But now my faith compels me to articulate a different path. A path often at cross-purposes with the world.

In our key text we find Jesus telling his disciples about his impending suffering and death. This revelation comes on the heels of Peter's famous confession that Jesus was the Christ (Matt. 16:16). Now Jesus was adding further clarification to his role as the Messiah. The Messiah must go to Jerusalem, suffer many things, and be killed. This was more than Peter could stand to hear. So, Peter intervened.

From Matthew's Gospel we know that it was Peter who was the first disciple called by Jesus (4:18). Peter was the first disciple named when Jesus commissioned them for service (10:2). It was Peter who dared to step out of the boat to walk on water with Jesus (14:29). And it was Peter who first confesses Jesus as the Christ (16:16). It is no surprise then for Peter to rebuke Jesus for this startling talk of suffering and death. "Peter took him aside and began to rebuke him. 'Never, Lord!' he said. 'This shall never happen to you!' " (NIV). Today we might say "God forbid!" Peter was not going to stand by and let his teacher and Lord be treated in this way. He once again assumes his leadership role among the disciples and rebukes Jesus! In his mind, this was the only logical thing to do. Someone had to protect Jesus from such thinking.

Jesus, however, was the one doing the rebuking that day. Recalling language from his wilderness temptations he says,

"Get behind me, Satan! You are a stumbling block to me; for you are setting your mind not on divine things but on human things." Peter, "the rock" who was going to build the church, is now Peter the stumbling block, tripping up the way of the Messiah and his followers. Peter, like many of us, didn't hear all of what Jesus was saying. Somehow he missed "and on the third day be raised." The Believers Church Bible Commentary for *Matthew* makes this observation about this text:

> From a worldly point of view, sacrificing one's life means a total and irretrievable loss. Accordingly, self-preservation becomes a high priority.[3]

Peter could not see past the "total and irretrievable loss" that Jesus spoke of. Neither could he anticipate the transforming power of the resurrection. He responded in a normal, human, and worldly way. But that was not the way of Jesus. Jesus goes on to say:

> If any want to become my followers, let them deny themselves and take up their cross and follow me. For those who want to save their life will lose it, and those who lose their life for my sake will find it. For what will it profit them if they gain the whole world but forfeit their life? Or what will they give in return for their life? (Matt. 16:24-26)

Are we ready to pick up our cross and follow Jesus? Having a "cross to bear" has been whittled down to putting up with an annoying co-worker or a debilitating illness or injury. While I don't want to trivialize in any way the real suffering of people, I'm not ready to concede that it is the same as following Christ to crucifixion. I believe that picking up our cross to follow Jesus means just what it says, picking up the cross. Trying to save our lives at all costs, Jesus said, means losing the real meaning of life in the kingdom. You might gain the whole world but lose your soul in the process. What price do you place on eternal life?

"What about you? Who do you say that I am?" Those are the questions Jesus put to his disciples in Matthew 16:15 which led to Peter's confession. It is striking that his confession of Christ is so closely linked to his rebuke. And yet, how many of us confess Jesus as Lord without really counting the cost? How many times have we sung the familiar camp song "I have decided to follow Jesus, No turning back, No turning back"? Saying YES to Jesus by definition puts us at odds with the ways of the world. Nonconformity with the world (Rom. 12:2) means following Christ in life and possibly our death. Mennonites like to quote the Anabaptist Hans Denk who said "No one may truly know Christ unless he follow him in life."[4]

Witness means martyr. We don't readily associate witnesses for Christ with martyrdom. In fact, the Greek word for witness in the New Testament *is* the word for martyr.[5]

As the early church suffered persecution, the term evolved into the meaning we commonly associate with it today. A simple illustration of this can be found by comparing the NIV translation of Acts 22:20 with the NRSV. The first makes reference to "your martyr Stephen" while the second says "your witness Stephen." Imagine the impact on our mission endeavors if we would substitute martyr for witness in Acts 1:8. "But you will receive power when the Holy Spirit has come upon you; and you will be my *witnesses (martyrs)* in Jerusalem, in all Judea and Samaria, and to the ends of the earth" (emphasis mine).

Jerusalem represented home for the disciples and the early church. It was the center of worship and Jewish life. In the great commission, Jerusalem meant your neighborhood, your hometown, your city of origin, your family and friends. Judea was the surrounding area that was also familiar. There were people "like us" who weren't all that different when they came to visit or we visited them. Pilgrims made their annual trek to Jerusalem for worship and celebration. Though strangers, they were not enemies. Samaria represented hostile territory. Skirmishes and theological battles raged for years between Jews and Samaritans not unlike the conflict in Northern Ireland. Protestants and Catholics live in separate neighborhoods, worship in different ways, and maintain long memories of distrust. So when Jesus said to witness starting at home and the surrounding area, that felt safe and doable. But when he said "to Samaria and to the ends of the earth" that meant something entirely different. That meant risk and confrontation. That meant going to places most of us take great pains to avoid. Many of us avoid cities or the country depending on where we feel comfortable, or people groups that speak a different language or otherwise are not like us. But Jesus and the gospel compel us to go there, to share our lives and our faith, to make a difference for the sake of the kingdom. That has always meant taking a calculated risk both spiritually and physically. What we know, and the kind of people we associate with, get stretched and broadened. They may reject our message and challenge our very presence. But we go in the name of Christ, with a message of hope and reconciliation and under the influence of the Holy Spirit.

"But you will receive power when the Holy Spirit has come upon you. . . ." Embracing the power of the Holy Spirit means harnessing the resurrection power of eternal life. That means that we don't hold so tenaciously to the material goods the world has to offer or to our present existence. And we can go into friendly or hostile territory under God's protection of resurrection hope. Jesus invites us to follow him . . . all the way.

Questions for Discussion
1. Can you identify with Peter only hearing Jesus talk of suffering and death and missing the resurrection?
2. How are we caught up in the "worldly way of thinking" regarding self-preservation?
3. What does costly discipleship mean in light of this text?
4. In what ways might we rebuke Jesus in our words or actions?

5. Where is Samaria for your church?
6. If Jesus' cross was for the salvation of the world, what would "taking up our cross" do for the world?

3
Symbol Choices

*Life is a journey toward God. This decides the
value and importance of anything and everything.
Christians are a people whose King is God, and
whose home is eternity, and who are strangers,
sojourners, and exiles in the world.*

—William Barclay[1]

Key Text *Philippians 2:5-11*

Let the same mind be in you that was in Christ Jesus, who,
though he was in the form of God, did not regard equality
with God as something to be exploited, but emptied himself,
taking the form of a slave, being born in human likeness.
And being found in human form, he humbled himself and
became obedient to the point of death—even death on a
cross. Therefore God also highly exalted him and gave him
the name that is above every name, so that at the name of
Jesus every knee should bend, in heaven and on earth and
under the earth, and every tongue should confess that Jesus
Christ is Lord, to the glory of God the Father.

Symbols are important to us because they point to something
or someone that has meaning in our lives. On the bulletin
board in my office is the Ohio State University logo. It reminds me of the scarlet and gray "Buckeyes" football team
that I have been rooting for since I was in Junior High School.
It's a symbol of my loyalty as a fan, of my native state, and of
the sports team I idolized in my youth. Now imagine a display
table with the following items: a picture book celebrating war
heroes (I have one from World War I) next to the *Martyrs Mirror*[2]; a wineglass and a communion cup; and a sand bucket,
debit card, and beach towel alongside a basin and towel. Let's

explore what these items symbolize, and keep in mind that it's not so much the objects themselves that are important but what they represent.

Defining our heroes. The book of war pictures and the *Martyrs Mirror* both tell about heroes, sacrifice, and shed blood. Both tell about people who were willing to make "the ultimate sacrifice." The book of war heroes sends the message that violence can be redemptive, that sometimes we have to choose the lesser of two evils. Change is brought about by "any means necessary." Violence, especially in war, is seen as redemptive because a greater purpose is accomplished and thus "redeems" the violence employed. The following tribute, "Dedicated to the American Fighting Man," was written by General John J. Pershing, Commander in Chief of the American Expeditionary Forces, on November 12, 1918, at the close of World War I.

> The enemy has capitulated. It is fitting that I address myself in thanks directly to the officers and soldiers of the American Expeditionary Forces who by their heroic efforts have made possible this glorious result. Our armies, hurriedly raised and hastily trained, met a veteran enemy, and by courage, discipline, and skill always defeated him. Without complaint you have endured incessant toil, privation, and danger. You have seen many of your comrades make the supreme sacrifice that freedom may live. I thank you for the patience and courage with which you have endured. I congratulate you upon the splendid fruits of victory which your heroism and the blood of our gallant dead are now presenting our nation. Your deeds will live forever on the most glorious pages of American history.[3]

The *Martyrs Mirror* tells a different story. Making "the supreme sacrifice" in war is to give your life for your country. In the context of faith, giving one's life means something different since we are not trying to have others give up their lives while risking ours. Christians through the centuries were burned at the stake, drowned, or otherwise executed because they would not relinquish their commitment to Jesus as Lord. Martyrdom is never something Christians seek but are always willing to embrace. Sacrifices are made not for country but for the kingdom of God. Stories of loss and heroism are themes running through both books, but there is a fundamental difference. Christians by definition are people who are never willing to take a life for any cause, but are always willing to die for the cause of Christ. Christ is our hero.

Which cup? The wineglass tempts us with the easy way out by drowning our sorrows and insulating ourselves from our own pain. It symbolizes our tendency to anesthetize our daily struggles with diversions and trivial pursuits, filling our days with work and our nights with pleasure. The multimillion dollar alcohol industry wants us to equate alcohol with happiness. The communion cup, on the other hand, represents the shed blood of Jesus. "This cup that is poured out for you is the new covenant in my blood" (Luke 22:20). Jesus resisted the easy ways of responding to the very real threats to his life. In the garden of Gethsemane he prayed "Father, if you are willing, remove this cup from me; yet, not my will but yours be done" (Luke 22:42). The cup Jesus referred to is the "cup of suffering,"[4] and he warned his disciples of its cost (Matt. 20:22-23). Jesus not only chose this cup, but drank deeply from it.

The song of the self or service? The song of the self is an egocentric refrain that shouts, "I am most important. I should have some nice things in life. I should be able to play when I feel like it. I want what I want when I want it." Sound familiar? Ours is an instant gratification society—a culture of multiple choices. Credit and debit cards allow for instant purchases and the Internet connects us to a range of choices previously unimaginable. Pastor-Poet Joyce Shutt wrote this "Consumers' Prayer."[5]

throwaway bottles	instant puddings
throwaway cans	instant rice
throwaway friendships	instant intimacy
throwaway fans	instant ice
disposable diapers	plastic dishes
disposable plates	plastic laces
disposable people	plastic flowers
disposable wastes	plastic faces

Lord of the living
transcending our lies
infuse us with meaning
recycle our lives

The beach towel, debit card, and sand bucket symbolize our lust for self-indulgence and instant gratification. By contrast, the basin and towel represent service to others. These too are symbols from the Last Supper of Jesus with his disciples (John 13:4-5). The Master serves the disciples in this humbling and menial task. Service is more than a short-term commitment to doing random acts of kindness for others. It's a way of life that shapes our view of the world and follows in the ways of Jesus. Service changes us.

Philippians 2:5-11 calls us to follow the example of Jesus. He had the power of God at his disposal but chose not to exploit that power to his own advantage. Instead, he humbled himself to become one of us and show us the ways of God in the flesh. The voluntary humility of Jesus is illustrated in the two triangles on the next page.[6]

The first triangle shows the stratified, pyramid of power in Jesus' day. Everyone had their place and it was very difficult to cross the established social barriers. Those at the top wielded power over those at the bottom through economic, political, and military leverage. The inverted pyramid of grace represents what Jesus accomplished according to Philippians 2.

Caesar Is Lord
Ruling Elite
Roman Troops
Roman Citizens
The Rich, Men
Middle Class
Religious Hierarchy
Women
Children
Day Laborers, Servants
Widows, Orphans, Aliens
Disabled, The Poor, Slaves
The Least of These

Pyramid of Power

Community of Equals

Jesus

**Inverted Pyramid
of Grace**

By overlaying the inverted pyramid of grace over the pyramid of power we see very quickly where Jesus, the foundation of the church, enters the world. He comes in the form of a servant and brings healing and hope to those who are "the least of these" (Matt. 25:40, 45). This is "power from below" where everyone is empowered to become part of and contribute to the whole. Jesus creates something that Caesar never could: a community of equals based not on power and position, but on love and a common commitment to God and God's kingdom. In the kingdom, Jesus is Lord, not Caesar. In the kingdom, Jesus creates community based on one common foundation. The first are last, weakness is strength, the poor inherit the earth, and children are model citizens. It is truly an upside-down kingdom.[7]

The inverted triangle encompasses the alternative symbols we examined earlier. The *Martyrs Mirror*, the communion cup, and the basin and towel all find a home in the inverted pyramid of grace in the community of equals created by Jesus. The symbols we choose to identify with reflect the values and core beliefs we hold sacred. For the follower of Jesus the symbols may look foolish or out of place in a sophisticated, materialistic world. But they are consistent with the faith we profess and the hero we worship. Let's not forget that the writer of Philippians invites us to have the same *attitude* as Christ Jesus. How we look at life, our circumstances, and matters of self-preservation essentially boils down to our attitude. By taking on the "mind of Christ" (1 Cor. 2:16) we begin to think and in turn translate our actions into the ways of Jesus. In so doing we conform ourselves to his attitude toward self-preservation.

Questions for Discussion

1. Which of the "symbol choices" was most challenging for you? Why?
2. Translate the "Pyramid of Power" into a modern stratification (e.g., president, Congress, etc. to homeless persons, AIDS sufferers, etc.). What implications does this have for where Jesus can be found in our society today?
3. Why is it so difficult to give up or change our attitude in matters of faith?
4. In what upside-down ways does your faith get expressed?
5. What did you find most helpful in Joyce Shutt's "Consumers' Prayer"? Add a verse.

4
Do You Believe This?

*Nothing is completely dead within us, so dead that it
cannot be raised. And this story puts the question:
What is the dead Lazarus within me? What part
have I allowed to die so that I am living only as a
partial human being, busy getting more and more set
in my own one-sidedness? I need to remember Jesus
can bring any part of us back to life.*

—Morton Kelsey[1]

Key Text *John 11:21-27*

Martha said to Jesus, "Lord, if you had been here, my brother would not have died. But even now I know that God will
give you whatever you ask of him." Jesus said to her, "Your
brother will rise again." Martha said to him, "I know that
he will rise again in the resurrection on the last day." Jesus
said to her, "I am the resurrection and the life. Those who
believe in me, even though they die, will live, and everyone
who lives and believes in me will never die. Do you believe
this?" She said to him, "Yes, Lord, I believe that you are the
Messiah, the Son of God, the one coming into the world."

I should have been there when my Grandmother Amstutz
died. It was a sunny Sunday afternoon and my best friend Tim
and I were riding through the rural Ohio countryside in his
parents '65 Mustang. Tim was a year older and had his driver's license. We enjoyed the new freedom that fact brought to
our lives and our friendship. We stopped at an overpass that
led to the nursing home where my grandmother was living. I
mentioned to Tim earlier that I was supposed to stop by to see
her. "Do you want to go now?" he asked. "No, I'll go some
other time." I said. Later that evening she died. Mom and Dad
told me that grandma had asked for me. I felt horrible. Grand-

mother and I were very close, especially when she lived with us on the farm. I enjoyed visiting her in the nursing home. So why didn't I go that Sunday? I learned an important lesson that day about not taking loved ones for granted. If only I would have gone.

The Gospel of John tells the story of the raising of Lazarus. We remember the dramatic resurrection story but too easily miss what led up to that defining moment in Jesus' ministry. If you go back to the beginning of chapter 11 you find that Jesus got word of Lazarus' illness in plenty of time to go and perhaps heal him while he was still alive. Why did Jesus deliberately delay? It seemed out of character for Jesus to not immediately go to his friend, but he had another purpose in mind. When, after two days, he did decided to return to Judea (v. 7f.) the disciples questioned the wisdom of that move (vv. 8-9). Jesus was faced with a personal safety issue. Was visiting a sick friend worth the risk? The Jews had earlier tried to stone him in Judea (John 10:31), a fact not lost on the disciples. Why risk another confrontation?

Jesus knew that his time had not yet come but the disciples had no way of knowing. Embracing the idea that Jesus may not be as lucky to escape the next time, one of the disciples made a bold statement. Thomas showed great courage when he said to the other disciples, "Let us also go, that we may die with him" (John 11:16). Peter made a similar statement of loyalty and sacrifice at the Last Supper (John 13:37), but Jesus already knew that Peter would chicken out in the end. Thomas is most famous for his doubting, but here he clearly demonstrated that he understood the cost of following Jesus. It was risky business to be around Jesus. Is it still so today?

The power of death is very strong and pervasive. It can so quickly overshadow life and overcome us with grief. Death is often unjust, untimely, and unfair. Death seems like the ultimate enemy. We fear our own death and the death of our loved ones. When death visited the home of Mary, Martha, and Lazarus, the sisters couldn't comprehend why Jesus was so late in coming. They had sent word in plenty of time, but he didn't come. He should have been there, but he wasn't. Don't we ask God the same questions? Why didn't you come? Where were you when we needed you most? Jesus could have healed Lazarus before he died, or at least said good-bye to him. "Lord, if you had been here, my brother would not have died" (John 11:21, 32). After *why* comes *if only*: If only we would have said something sooner. If only he would have gone to the doctor yesterday. If only he would have taken his medication as directed. If only I would have gone to see grandma as I had promised.

It wasn't lack of compassion. We know that Jesus didn't tarry because he didn't care. After talking with Mary, Jesus wept. But why did he weep? This may hold the key to why he didn't arrive sooner. Perhaps Jesus was moved to tears by the *power* death had over the sisters and mourners. Here was an opportunity to demonstrate the greater power of God over death *even if Jesus was not physically present*. In this story, Jesus encountered life at its most vulnerable place: the moment when we feel the most helpless and powerless against a force so devastating, so indiscriminate, so permanent. A time was coming soon when Jesus would no longer be with them physically, and yet he would be *present* among them, within them. Jesus prepared his followers to live in the new reality demonstrated in the raising of Lazarus. The power of resurrection is still at work. Theologian Sandra M. Schneiders writes:

> Jesus' delay, like his physical absence before the Parousia, is real; and the suffering it causes is real. Jesus does not rebuke the sisters for their suffering, either at their brother's death or at Jesus' absence. What he demands is that they, and all the disciples, realize and believe in his intimate real presence in and through his physical absence. This presence can sustain believers through all the sufferings of this life, even death itself.[2]

As believers today we count on this promise and paradox. When a Christian dies we do what people of faith have done for two thousand years. We grieve for what we feel and rejoice for what we know. We call on the grace of God and the saving power of Jesus Christ to transform the sting of death into victory. Resurrection makes all the difference.

Do you believe this? When Martha articulates the "If only" lament, Jesus makes a statement that was somewhat lost on Martha. "Your brother will rise again" (John 11:23). Martha said to him, "I know that he will rise again in the resurrection on the last day" (v. 24). Jesus clarifies his meaning with one of the most important truths about the resurrection and Christian faith. Jesus said to her, "I am the resurrection and the life. Those who believe in me, even though they die, will live, and everyone who lives and believes in me will never die. Do you believe this?" (vv. 25-26). Here the living paradox of our faith comes to life. Jesus IS the resurrection and the life. Even though he is not here, he IS here. Listen to what he said when he ascended into heaven. "And remember, I am with you always, to the end of the age" (Matt. 28:20b). Do we believe that?

Believing in Jesus means our old way of understanding death is transformed by the gift of eternal life. Those who accept its gift receive its power and embrace eternal life. They never die. Challenging the assumption of self-preservation begins right here for the follower of Jesus Christ. Jesus took a calculated risk to come back to Judea in the face of open hostility from the Jews. Thomas was ready to make the ultimate sacrifice of a disciple for the sake of his Master. Martha implicitly believes in Jesus even though she doesn't always understand him. Therein lies the challenge. Can we do the same? Can we, by the power of the Holy Spirit and the promise of the resurrection, take calculated risks for the sake of the kingdom?

Taking the question seriously. Do we believe it? If we do, what does that mean regarding self-preservation at all costs? How do we live within that promise? What opportunities are open to us that are new and previously rejected out of hand? Dare we leave hearth and home for ministry areas most consider too risky? How does the resurrection not only transform our belief about our physical death but transform our physical life as well? I believe that Jesus is calling all of his followers to re-define our life/death parameters. Resurrection is for now.

What binds us? The actual raising of Lazarus is almost inci-dental to John 11. Occupying only seven of the fifty-seven verses, it hardly commands center stage. True, it is a dramat-ic and culminating event in Jesus' public ministry, but perhaps not the main point of the story. When Lazarus does come forth from the tomb he is still bound by the burial cloths. He is bound hand and foot by the trappings of death. His resur-rection was temporal, he would die a physical death again. We can only imagine the joy Mary and Martha and their friends experienced that day. "Unbind him, and let him go" (v. 44) was the final instruction Jesus gave regarding Lazarus. How often are we bound and immobilized by death? Death of a loved one? Death of a relationship? Death due to loss of in-come, mobility, job, ideology? As Morton Kelsey observes "I need to remember Jesus can bring any part of us back to life"[3] Do you believe this? That is the question.

Questions for Discussion
1. When have you ever felt that "you should have been there"?
2. Read the quote at the beginning of the chapter from Morton Kelsey again. Have you experienced resurrection in this sense?
3. Jesus is the resurrection and the life. How has this faith promise been made real for you? How do you live out this belief?

4. How is Jesus present in our reality even though he is not physically there?
5. Jesus risked his personal safety to bring new life to Lazarus. How can Christians do the same today?
6. What is binding your life, like Lazarus' grave clothes, which Jesus could release?

5
The Cross and Community

*To be or not to be a community is not an option
for the church. By nature the church is a community
and experiences communion. But the question before
the people of God is: What kind of community will
we be?*

—John Driver[1]

Key Text *1 Corinthians 12:12-14, 27*
For just as the body is one and has many members, and all
the members of the body, though many, are one body, so it is
with Christ. For in the one Spirit we were all baptized into
one body—Jews or Greeks, slaves or free—and we were all
made to drink of one Spirit. Indeed, the body does not con-
sist of one member but of many. . . .

Now you are the body of Christ and individually members
of it.

During my seminary years I helped organize a new student
K-group (K for *koinonia*, Greek for community). We became
accountable to one another in all aspects of our lives, especially as we processed our various calls to ministry. We stayed
together all three years and have met for a week of vacation
every year since 1984. Randy and Ann, Dave and Essie, Roger
and Cynthia, and Lorraine and I became a basic Christian
community and stay in touch by e-mail. Prior to the electron-
ic communication revolution we each wrote a page in a circle
letter, not unlike the pastoral letters of Paul to the early
church. We share our joys and sorrows, our failures and challenges. Our definition of family is extended to include each
other and our children. Because of our long and sustained his-

tory together, we easily pick up where we left off when we are physically together. This experience, more than any other in my Christian life, has convinced me of the power and spiritual necessity of small groups. What we forged in the early, formative years in our seminary studies set the stage for our ongoing love and concern for each other. We have been conscious of not excluding others and have often invited other mutual friends to join us. But the essential trust and depth of our relationships remain vital to our respective ministries despite the fact that we are separated by vast geographical distances. "For where two or three are gathered in my name, I am there among them" (Matt. 18:20). Christian community for me is not an abstract concept. It was and is made real by the brothers and sisters in Christ that "Rejoice with those who rejoice, weep with those who weep" (Rom. 12:15).

That mutual accountability in Christian community by definition informs our approach to self-preservation at all costs. Self-preservation at face value is *self*-centered. I am protecting *my* life, or *my* property, or *my* loved ones from lethal violence and make the decision *on my own* to engage lethal violence to do so. Basic Christian community calls us to challenge that self-centered assumption.

> It is an altruistic form of egoism when I defend *my* wife or *my* child because they are precisely *my own*. . . . Thus this becomes an act of selfishness; though covered over with the halo of service to others, it is still self-oriented in its structure. . . . True, the potential victim is my neighbor and thus deserving of my help. But the attacker also becomes at that moment a neighbor, and any attempt to distinguish between these two and say that the nearness of my family member as preferred neighbor takes precedence over that of my attacker is also a form of egoism.[2]

We are all members of one body, Paul tells us, and Christ is the head of the body, the church. Doesn't it seem logical that the members of the body should listen to what the head is saying about self-preservation? Doesn't the body also have an obligation to take seriously what message it is sending to the rest of the body? Jesus leads by example. When he was faced with life-threatening situations in life he did so under the protection of God and in trust of the resurrection. Since he had not faced his own death and resurrection before, he had to trust that God was going to keep his promises. It is the same invitation that God extends to us as God's children, only this time we also have someone who has led the way. As people of faith, living and manifesting the body of Christ in our world, we too are faced with situations that threaten our very lives. Why is it then that we ignore the example of Jesus and deny the instructions of our head? Jesus prayed in the garden, "Yet not what I want but what you want."

We also must wrestle with the assumption that those in whose name we are ready to defend by lethal violence *want* to be defended in this way. John Howard Yoder argues convincingly that this is not always the case.

> The person who is being attacked (my wife or mother or daughter) is also a responsible being and should be part of my decision-making process. If this person shares my values then she would be guided by some of the same considerations which guide me. It would be certainly improper for me as a third party in the conflict to deal with her enemy in a way she would not desire. At least some Christian women would not want to be protected by lethal violence.[3]

Mennonites as a community of faith have taken the nonviolent way of Jesus as a community core value. When you join a Mennonite church and embrace the collective history and current theological understanding of the biblical way of peace, you are joining a community that does not want to be defended by lethal violence. Mennonite churches in North America have differing practices on whether the willingness to use lethal force is a test of one's church membership. Yet churches that do not make this a test of membership still make this teaching a core belief and ask that members be willing to be led in this direction. The *Confession of Faith in a Menno-nite Perspective* says:

> As disciples of Christ, we do not prepare for war, or participate in war or military service. The same Spirit that empowered Jesus also empowers us to love enemies, to forgive rather than to seek revenge, to practice right relationships, to rely on the community of faith to settle disputes, and to resist evil without violence.[4]

The teaching and accountability of the community we join constrains us from acting alone on the issue of self-preservation at all costs. As we will examine in a later chapter, there are active ways Christians committed to nonviolence can resist evil consistent with the teachings of Christ. I have always argued that I would personally interpose myself against any would-be attacker of my family. I would be willing (as far as I can envision such a scenario) to sacrifice myself on behalf of my wife and children, but I would not use a gun or lethal force to do so. If my daughter wanders onto a busy road and I run and push her out of the path of an oncoming driver I have used force to save her life. She may even suffer a broken arm in the process. I did not, however, shoot the driver with a rifle to stop him from running over my loved one. I may even be fatally wounded in the rescue attempt, but I have not done any harm to the driver of the vehicle.

The community out of which I live my life supports my decision to embrace nonviolence as the way to incarnate my Christian beliefs. It is a radical faith decision forged in the crucible of persecution and martyrdom among the early Anabaptists,[5] and affirmed in the witness and testimony among Mennonites and other Anabaptist groups today. Each generation must decide to embrace and perpetuate this understanding of discipleship as its own. Just as Christian faith itself is always one generation away from extinction, so it is with Christ's way of peace. We do not inherit pacifism and nonviolence anymore than we can inherit baptism or salvation. The conditions can be created for that decision to be a positive one on both accounts but it is not made for us. We must choose to claim Christ's way of peace as a core value and basic tenet of our faith. And because we understand the nature of the church to be a teaching and nurturing community we do not make this crucial decision in isolation. The community helps to shape our decision for peace and nurture and sustain it along the way.

Community discernment is also at work on a much broader scale than the small group or congregation. During the fall of 2000, Mennonites in the United States were invited to stand in solidarity with our Anabaptist brothers and sisters in Colombia. Church leaders called on Christians around the world to pray for an end to the violence and for U.S. Christians in particular to challenge the recent U.S. Government decision to send $1.3 billion into Colombia, mostly in military aid. Mennonite leader Ricardo Esquivia was direct in his plea, "Through your tax dollars, you are supporting war."[6] I was serving as chair of the Commission on Home Ministries for the General Conference Mennonite Church at the time. Meeting in joint sessions with the Mennonite Board of Missions, the Commission on Overseas Missions, and the Ministries Commission of Mennonite Church, Canada, our respective boards took action to send a letter of solidarity to the Mennonite churches in Colombia. I was glad to add my personal signature to the letter and did so as an act of community.

Mission worker Bonnie Klassen gave a moving account of her daily encounters with violence in Colombia as assistant director of *JustaPaz* in Bogota. This is the Mennonite Church of Colombia's peace and justice agency and is directed by Ricardo Esquivia. Klassen, from Kitchener, Ontario, shared how living in one of the most violent societies in the world, and knowing that friends and acquaintances are under death threats, has taught her a difficult lesson in patience. In a follow-up interview, Klassen said:

> I believe in what goes beyond human effort. I believe in resurrection. God can act, bring life, transform a situation. Christ's

resurrection opened up all the doors to make everything new. One of the principal roles of the church is to bring hope. People who are desperate all over the world believe violence is the only solution. The church needs to keep people from reaching that point [of desperation].[7]

It was the Christian community that sent Bonnie from North America to serve in Colombia, knowing that she faces very real dangers along with her brothers and sisters in the faith in Bogota. Christ's way of peace, growing out of the community context of faith, compels us to share not only in the suffering of Colombian Christians, but also in resurrection hope.

Questions for Discussion

1. How has "family" been defined in your life?
2. How does our participation and membership in a faith community influence our protection of our nuclear family?
3. How can our faith community help us strengthen our resolve to find an alternative to lethal violence?
4. How do you understand the distinction between force and violence? Can you think of ways the use of force is ever justified?
5. Are there people in your group who have faced personal safety issues? How was the situation resolved? How did faith influence his or her actions?
6. Do Mennonites in North America see themselves as "radicals" today? Can you think of other examples of how community transcends national borders for peace and justice?

6

The Cross and Hospitality

Kindling the Fire[1]

*This morning, as I kindle the fire upon my
hearth, I pray that the flame of God's
love may burn in my heart, and the
hearts of all I meet today.*

*I pray that no envy and malice, no hatred or
fear, may smother the flame.*

*I pray that indifference and apathy,
contempt and pride, may not pour like
cold water on the fire.*

*Instead, may the spark of God's love light
the love in my heart, that it may burn
brightly through the day.*

*And may I warm those that are lonely,
whose hearts are cold and lifeless, so that
all may know the comfort of God's love.*

Key Texts Romans 5:10; Psalm 23

For if while we were enemies, we were reconciled to God
through the death of his Son, much more surely, having been
reconciled, will we be saved by his life.

The LORD is my shepherd, I shall not want. He makes me lie
down in green pastures; he leads me beside still waters; he
restores my soul. He leads me in right paths for his name's
sake. Even though I walk through the darkest valley, I fear
no evil; for you are with me; your rod and your staff—they
comfort me. You prepare a table before me in the presence
of my enemies; you anoint my head with oil; my cup over-

flows. Surely goodness and mercy shall follow me all the days of my life, and I shall dwell in the house of the LORD my whole life long.

Hospitality in our day and age is normally associated with hosting people in our home. It means preparing a meal or planning a party. Hospitality for my family has always meant we give the house a good cleaning. We can always tell when it's time to invite someone over by whether the kitchen floor needs scrubbing or the living room dusted. Hospitality means get busy!

Entertaining strangers is something Paul encouraged the Christians in Rome to do. In Romans 12:13 he says, "Contribute to the needs of the saints; extend hospitality to strangers." In Greek, the word for hospitality is a compound word *philoxenos*, which literally means brotherly love for strangers. It is one thing to invite friends and neighbors over for tea or a dinner party. But what about strangers? Sojourners and strangers were often travelers who needed a place to lodge or a hot meal. In the biblical tradition this transient group was to be looked after with special care and protection. God instructs the newly liberated Jews to do so because of their own experience of living in a foreign land. "You shall also love the stranger, for you were strangers in the land of Egypt" (Deut. 10:19). In the New Testament a divine identification with strangers is evident in the judgment scene of Matthew 25:31f. "For I was hungry and you gave me food, I was thirsty and you gave me something to drink, I was a stranger and you welcomed me. . . ." The writer of Hebrews affirms this understanding of hosting the divine in 13:2 "Do not neglect to show hospitality to strangers, for by doing that some have entertained angels without knowing it." Hospitality emerges as a way of remembering who we are as a pilgrim people, and as a way of honoring God. Asked how she could continue working with the "untouchables" in India, Mother Teresa replied,

"When I hold a dying person in my arms I see the face of Jesus."[2]

Hospitality as refuge. Paul minces no words when he says, "For if while we were enemies, we were reconciled to God through the death of his Son, much more surely, having been reconciled, will we be saved by his life" (Rom. 5:10). It rattles us to think that our sin so separates us from God that we become God's enemies. In spite of that fact, God demonstrates such love for us in Jesus Christ. God's way of dealing with enemies was to send his Son to die on their behalf and extend them eternal life. Does that make sense? It does when we understand just how deep and vast and beyond all human understanding the love of God in Christ Jesus truly is. Another illustration of God's love for us is that one line in Psalm 23 that never seemed very clear before. What does the psalmist mean by "You prepare a table before me in the presence of my enemies"? The following interpretation helps shed new light on its meaning.

> In the second part of the psalm (vv. 5-6) the imagery shifts to the shepherd as host. According to the bedouin law of hospitality, once a traveler is received into the shepherd's tent, and especially once his host has spread food before him, he is guaranteed immunity from enemies who may be attempting to overtake him. In pastoral circles no human protection is greater than that afforded by the hospitality of a bedouin chief. So the psalmist expresses his trust in the Good Shepherd by saying that in Yahweh's tent he finds a protecting and gracious welcome. This divine hospitality is not just a temporary reprieve but a limitless protection from the powers that threaten his existence.[3]

God's gracious and generous hospitality is first extended to us when we are estranged and even militant toward God. We are extended an invitation as a sojourner and stranger to enter into God's tent of protection. God sets before us a meal to nourish both body and soul. When we become God's children, living under God's loving protection, both now and for all eternity, can we do anything less than extend that same loving hospitality to those we meet, including our enemies?

Hospitality as reconciliation. In 2 Kings 6:8 we are told that "the king of Aram was at war with Israel." Because Elisha was able to know the plans of the king of Aram, his maneuvers were repeatedly preempted. The king of Aram was outraged and sent horses and chariots and a great army to try and seize Elisha. Once again, God aided Elisha and the soldiers are miraculously blinded and led into Samaria. The Lord opens the eyes of the soldiers and they are surrounded. What happens next?

> When the king of Israel saw them he said to Elisha, "Father, shall I kill them? Shall I kill them?" He answered, "No! Did you capture with your sword and your bow those whom you want to kill? Set food and water before them so that they may eat and drink; and let them go to their master" (2 Kings 6:21-22).

Did this profoundly unexpected show of hospitality turn the tide in the ongoing battle with the Arameans? The text does not say. But we do know that "the Arameans no longer came raiding into the land of Israel" (v. 23). Perhaps it was the fantastic show of divine power that made the king of Aram afraid to take on the Israelites again. On the other hand, it may have been the totally unexpected act of kindness and hospitality that reversed the course of hostilities. In the book of Proverbs (25:21-22) we have this tidbit of wisdom to consider: "If your enemies are hungry, give them bread to eat; and if they are thirsty, give them water to drink; for you will heap coals of fire on their heads, and the LORD will reward you." Paul quotes this wisdom saying in his discussion of overcoming evil with good in Romans 12:20, a theme we will examine in a later chapter. These are powerful images of meeting hostility with kindness, hostile intent with hospitality. It may in fact so disarm the enemy that hostilities will cease. That's what happens between God and us, so who can say the same power of God cannot transform hostilities between human enemies?

We fear the unknown. Strangers are people we don't know. The biblical view is that they are "friends we haven't met yet." What does the Bible story tell us about how to approach the unknown person in our midst? We teach our children to stay away from strangers. We know that it is a big risk to pick up a hitchhiker or to even stop to help a stranded motorist. Random violence in North America has altered the climate of how strangers are treated. How many of us really know our neighbors? Sadly, many of us are too frightened of the unknown to risk finding out. And yet, God persistently calls us to overcome our fears and extend the same "brotherly love toward strangers" that was extended to us. We may encounter resistance or even open hostility. But don't we have an equal chance of entertaining an angel? or Jesus? Who should we give the benefit of the doubt to?

The story is told of the missionary wife in China who was alone with her children during a spring drought. Some local militants said the gods were angry because foreigners had come into the city. There had never been a drought before they came to live in the city, therefore the gods were angry. Overhearing a plan to storm the missionary house at midnight, a trusted Chinese friend, Wang Amah, came to warn her employers. Andrew was away from home on a missionary assignment so Carie developed a plan should the attack occur. As midnight approached, Carie and Wang Amah prepared tea and cake. They swept the dining room and set the table and chairs as if preparing for guests. Carie then went to the door of the courtyard where the mob had gathered and threw open the front gate. Leaving the door wide open she turned up the oil lamp in the dining room and woke up the children. She dressed them and brought them downstairs to play with their toys.

Armed with sticks, clubs, and knives the angry men pressed into the courtyard of the house. Carie went to the door and called out, "Come in, friends, neighbors, I have tea prepared." Carie handed a cup of tea to the leader of the group and apologized for not having enough seats for everyone. Her son became frightened and ran to her side. She reassured the children, gently saying, "Nothing to be afraid of, darlings. Just some people come to see what we look like— such funny people, who want to see what Americans look like! They haven't seen Americans before." The crowd pressed into the dining room and noticed she was not afraid. "Why should I fear my neighbors?" she asked. The men examined the furniture, the curtains, the organ. One touched a note and Carie showed him how to make the sound come. Then she slipped into the seat and began to play softly and to sing, in Chinese, "Jesus, Thy Name I Love." The room fell silent until she finished. The men looked at each other. One muttered, "There is nothing here—only this woman, and these children—." "I go home," said another and went out. Others lingered and the leader halted to look at the children. He offered his hand to little Arthur who smiled and seized the man's forefinger. The man laughed and said, "Here is a good one to play." After examining the curious American toys and playing with the children, the leader finally rose and announced loudly, "There is nothing more to do here, I go home."

The others filed out, one by one through the courtyard and out the front gate. Carie slumped into a chair, exhausted. She picked up the baby and rocked him gently. Some men lingered at the gate and watched her. Carie went outside to close the gate and felt a cool southeast wind. After putting the children to bed Carie fell at last into a light sleep. She awoke to the sound of rain pouring on the tile roof, streaming from the corners of the house, and splashing upon the stones of the courtyard.[4]

Paul reminds us that while we were God's enemies, God took the initiative to offer reconciliation to us through Jesus

Christ. Doesn't that tell us something vitally important about the character of God? It doesn't just say that we were disobedient toward God like errant children. We were God's *enemies*. God could have destroyed us or cut us off from his love. Instead we were invited into God's tent of protection to find reconciliation, fellowship, and hospitality. As God's children, God's beloved, we reflect the loving character of God when we practice Christian hospitality to our neighbors, to strangers, and our enemies.[5]

Questions for Discussion

1. How has hospitality been a part of your experience? Have you ever entertained strangers? Enemies?

2. Explain how "brotherly love toward strangers" might help us deepen our commitment to practicing Christian hospitality.

3. Revisit Psalm 23:5-6. Does this explanation of God's hospitality ring true to your understanding of the text?

4. Was the ending of the story in 2 Kings 6 a surprise to you? Would such an unexpected turn of events be effective today?

5. Share other "victories without violence" that you know of from reading or personal experience.

6. How does extending hospitality to strangers and enemies reflect the character of God?

7
Who Is the Enemy?

The oil of religion should never be used
to increase the flames of violence. But
the oil of religion should always be used
as a soothing balm to heal the wounds of people.

—Luke Veronis, Albania[1]

Key Texts *Ephesians 6:12*

For our struggle is not against enemies of blood and flesh,
but against the rulers, against the authorities, against the
cosmic powers of this present darkness, against the spiritual
forces of evil in the heavenly places.

Luke 9:51-56

When the days drew near for him to be taken up, he set his
face to go to Jerusalem. And he sent messengers ahead of
him. On their way they entered a village of the Samaritans to
make ready for him; but they did not receive him, because
his face was set toward Jerusalem. When his disciples James
and John saw it, they said, "Lord, do you want us to command fire to come down from heaven and consume them?"
But he turned and rebuked them. Then they went on to
another village.

Christians believe that all people are created in God's image.
If that is so, why do some people act so terribly? In 1977
Ugandan Dictator Idi Amin was at the height of his terror.
Thousands of innocents were being brutally murdered and
tortured. *Campus Life*, a popular evangelical magazine for
youth, ran a provocative feature article titled, "Would You
Kill Idi Amin?"[2] Thirteen prominent evangelical Christian
leaders were asked to give their response to this question. The
majority of the respondents gave a qualified "no" saying they

may not personally be able to take Amin's life, though they wish someone would. Jay Kesler, then president of Youth for Christ, said, "Knowing my own personality, I'd have to say, yes, I would probably kill him." He later adds, "I would call upon God for his mercy and grace as my only possible hope of redemption."[3]

Two gave an unequivocal "no" expressing God's love for enemies and that Christians use weapons of love and reconciliation, not hatred and war. Both men were Ugandan refugees, one telling of how his life had been threatened by Amin's secret police during a worship service. How ironic that those closest to the violence, who had suffered personally from Amin's terror, were the clearest in their Christian pacifist convictions.[4] What these men articulated was a different way of defining enemies.

The real fight. Paul says that the real battle is not against flesh and blood but against the principalities and powers of this dark world. The ancient worldview went something like this. The earth was a floating disk on an endless and chaotic sea. The "heavens" (plural), were in two levels. What we call the atmosphere was where the principalities and powers resided. The spirit world was taken for granted and evil forces were out and about in the first layer of the heavenlies. God resided above that in the upper heavens, the second level. Hell, then, was not below but above, separating us from God. Paul said it's those malevolent forces that we need to be on guard against. Listen to what Jesus told his disciples when he sent them out on their first mission assignment. "Do not fear those who kill the body but cannot kill the soul; rather fear him who can destroy both soul and body in hell" (Matt. 10:28). There were structural and systemic forces at work that were beyond individual enemies. The Roman Empire was more than just a particular governor or soldier who persecuted the Jews and early Christians. It was an unjust societal structure that oppressed those without voice or vote. Can Christians today embrace the idea that other human beings are not the enemy?

Fire from heaven. Luke 9:51-54 finds Jesus and the disciples heading for Jerusalem. Galilee, where Jesus was from, and Jerusalem, where he was headed, were separated by Samaria. Conflicts between Jews and Samaritans were well known even though the Samaritans held the first five books of the Bible as sacred and claimed a common patriarchal heritage.[5] We are familiar with the woman at the well, the Samaritan leper, and the so-called "good" Samaritan.[6] That the messengers who were sent on ahead were rejected was no surprise. James and John were ready to put the Samaritans in their place and asked Jesus "Lord, do you want us to command fire to come down from heaven and consume them?" Notice the footnote in your Bible: "Other ancient authorities add 'as Elijah did.'" Elijah, you'll recall, was the fiery prophet who not only called down fire from heaven to defeat the prophets of Baal (1 Kings 18:38), but later destroyed the messengers sent by the king of Samaria (2 Kings 1:10)! James and John were simply following biblical and prophetic precedent. They knew God was on the side of Jesus. So why not destroy the enemy the old-fashioned way? But Jesus turned and rebuked them, with some manuscripts adding "You do not know what spirit you are of, for the Son of Man has not come to destroy the lives of human beings but to save them." And they went on to another village.

An important lesson. Jesus gives us an important lesson on how his followers are to respond to opposition. Were the disciples out of line to want to take revenge on the Samaritans? That's a different spirit, Jesus says. "If you want to follow me then understand what Spirit I'm about. My purpose is to save people's lives, not destroy them." Ouch. A rebuke from Jesus is never pleasant. Just ask Peter or James and John. The Spirit of Jesus is not one of employing lethal violence by calling down fire from heaven to destroy the enemy. His Spirit was to reconcile those enemies to God, to change people's lives, and to transform their hearts in obedience to God's will, in a word to save them, not destroy them. But did they get it? Do the disciples ever catch on to what Jesus was not only teaching them but demonstrating? Even at the point of Jesus' arrest we find one of them grabbing a sword and wounding the high priest's servant (Matt. 26:51). But church history tells us that for the first three hundred years the early Christians were not only pacifist but persecuted. Is it just coincidence that when the first Christians were most at risk they were the most like Jesus?

I'll never forget the huge stained-glass window in one of the stairwells of the Pentagon. Delton Franz from the MCC Washington Office was conducting one of his Washington Seminars that included a visit to the military headquarters of the United States. As we came around the corner and entered the staircase the scene depicted couldn't be missed. A man in full military dress uniform is kneeling in prayer at an altar, his family in their Sunday finest devoutly beside him. The caption was from Isaiah 6:8 "'Whom shall I send, and who will go for us?' And I said, 'Here am I; send me!'" That was a teachable moment in my coming to terms with how the United States mixes religion with military might. Were the wars fought by the United States military holy wars? Was answering the call of Uncle Sam synonymous with answering God's call? Was the fire called down upon Hiroshima and Nagasaki on August 6 and 9, 1945, God's judgment upon our enemies? Were those nuclear weapons blessed by God as they rained down upon men, women, and children who were deemed our enemies?

Let's revisit the principalities and powers question. Who are our enemies? Remember the ancient worldview that had the forces of evil above us? Paul's words in Ephesians 2:14 take on new meaning with this worldview in mind, "For he himself is our peace, who has made the two one and has destroyed the barrier, the dividing wall of hostility" (NIV). Jesus breaks through the power of evil and the enemy forces that stand be-

tween God and us. God and God's power to overcome evil
with good is accessible through Jesus Christ. That makes all
the difference when we're confronted with questions like,
"Would you kill Idi Amin?"

Wanting what God wants. If God's desire is to reconcile
everyone to kingdom ways, and if Jesus modeled a different
Spirit when dealing with enemies, then we as people of faith
need to rethink our view of enemies. Yes, real people do in-
credibly evil and terrible things to other people. And yes, there
is a proper place for evil to be stopped and restrained which
we will examine further in later chapters. The point I believe
Paul is making and Jesus is demonstrating is that for Christians, ends and means must be compatible. We don't kill people in order to save them.

Questions for Discussion
1. How would you respond to the Idi Amin question?
   (Substitute a current name.)
2. What correlation do you see between persecution and
   challenging self-preservation?
3. Does the ancient worldview help clarify how we redefine
   our enemies? Are we moderns too far removed from the
   spiritual dimension?
4. Were you surprised at the rebuke Jesus gave James and
   John for wanting to call down fire to destroy the enemy?
   How do we call down fire from heaven today?
5. What other ways does our government and/or military
   seek to bless their actions?
6. How might keeping ends and means compatible with
   Christ's way of peace force us into making difficult
   choices about our vocation?

8

Saved from Our Enemies

That word above all earthly powers,
No thanks to them, abideth.
The Spirit and the gifts are ours,
Through him who with us sideth:
Let goods and kindred go,

This mortal life also;
The body they may kill,

God's truth abideth still;
His kingdom is forever.[1]

—Martin Luther

Key Texts: *Psalm 46*

God is our refuge and strength, a very present help in trouble. Therefore we will not fear, though the earth should change, though the mountains shake in the heart of the sea; though its waters roar and foam, though the mountains tremble with its tumult. Selah. There is a river whose streams make glad the city of God, the holy habitation of the Most High. God is in the midst of the city; it shall not be moved; God will help it when the morning dawns. The nations are in an uproar, the kingdoms totter; he utters his voice, the earth melts. The LORD of hosts is with us; the God of Jacob is our refuge. Selah. Come, behold the works of the LORD; see what desolations he has brought on the earth. He makes wars cease to the end of the earth; he breaks the bow, and shatters the spear; he burns the shields with fire. "Be still, and know that I am God! I am exalted among the nations, I am exalted in the earth." The LORD of hosts is with us; the God of Jacob is our refuge.

Luke 1:68
Blessed be the Lord God of Israel, for he has looked favorably on his people and redeemed them. He has raised up a mighty savior for us in the house of his servant David, as he spoke through the mouth of his holy prophets from of old, that we would be saved from our enemies and from the hand of all who hate us.

When our daughter graduated from nursery school all the proud parents and siblings gathered in the large sanctuary of the church that also ran the school. After the host pastor opened with prayer we were all asked to please stand and recite the Pledge of Allegiance. There was an American flag on one side of the sanctuary and on the other a Christian flag. I stood out of respect but I did not pledge. When I got home that evening I wrote a letter to the director of the nursery school expressing my concern about the Pledge of Allegiance. Why was the Pledge of Allegiance a part of a Christian nursery school program, and in the sanctuary? If it was about memorization then why not Psalm 23 or the Lord's Prayer? The reply came back several weeks later after a special board meeting. "Readiness for kindergarten" was the answer.

This experience triggered a vigorous discussion in a young adult Sunday school class I was teaching the same year. We discussed the Pledge of Allegiance and the National Anthem. Did anyone really pay attention to the words? Most in the class admitted, "I never really thought about the words. I just do it automatically." Together we recited the words, first to the Pledge of Allegiance and then the National Anthem. I asked, "Do we, as people of faith, really want to celebrate 'The rocket's red glare, the bombs bursting in air'? Can we confess Jesus as Lord and still pledge our allegiance to the flag?" I told them personal stories of standing in the back of the room when I was a substitute teacher in public schools where the Pledge of Allegiance was part of the morning routine. I would stand out of respect but I would not place my hand upon my heart nor say the words. I do the same thing at ball games when the National Anthem is sung. To me the words matter. They matter to my faith and the practice of that faith.

Sung without thinking. How often do we find ourselves singing a hymn without really focusing on the words? We enjoy the music and the familiarity helps us worship and feel at home in church. But what about the words? What are we *saying* while we are singing? Luther's familiar hymn "A Mighty Fortress Is Our God" has a surprise ending. John Howard Yoder writes:

> Where the English translation says, "Let goods and kindred go; this mortal life also," the German says, "They seize wife and child; let it take its course!" This is not mere poetic exaggeration on Luther's part. Martin Luther taught nonresistance on the personal level. He believed that violence was permissible only at the behest of a legitimate government in a just cause.[2]

With how much certainty and conviction do we sing those words? Or is it just automatic? How much do we trust God to save us from our enemies? John Stoner has observed that Christians have no trouble in trusting God to save us from our sins, but rarely do we trust God to save us from our enemies. "Our confession is that, although we can no more save ourselves from our enemies than we can save ourselves from our sins, God offers through Jesus Christ to save us from both."[3] How does God save us from our enemies?

Psalm 46 is representative of the theology of God's protection. It professes that God is still the most powerful force in the universe and because we believe that we will not fear. How much of the violence we incur or threaten is based on fear? Fear of personal harm or injury, fear of the loss of our possessions or land, fear of being displaced, fear of death. "God is our refuge and strength, a very present help in trouble" (46:1). Do we really believe that? If so, how does that influence our view of self-preservation? Do we keep protective weapons in the house? Do we go to great expense and extremes to insure that our "goods and kindred" will never be harmed or damaged? Have we come to grips with how our "way of life" is protected by lethal violence or its threat? Where is the balance between common sense and Christian conviction?

God's disarmament project begins with us as people of faith. "He makes wars cease to the end of the earth; he breaks the bow, and shatters the spear; he burns the shields with fire" (46:9). We discussed in chapter 7 that other human beings are not the enemy. The real fight is against sin and evil. But as Christians we proclaim every Sunday that Jesus Christ is Lord; on the cross Christ conquered sin and death and overcame Satan. Easy to say, hard to follow. Sitting in the Mennonite Central Committee house in San Salvador on New Year's Eve 1983, I asked my friend Ron Flickinger how he copes with the danger to his own security. I was on a working vacation for ten days, sharing information about conscientious objection with Mennonite Church leaders in Honduras and Guatemala, and visiting MCC friends along the way. "We take calculated risks," said Ron.

That winter two MCC nurses were preparing for a new assignment in the conflictive zone. They asked, "Why should we only help those on the government-controlled side of the conflict? Isn't our mission to help *anyone* in need? People in the contested area also need medical assistance." Reluctantly, the MCC Central American department and headquarters staff authorized the new placement. It was a calculated risk.[4] That evening as firecrackers ushered in the New Year we talked about putting feet to our faith. In the morning we were told that not all the sounds we heard were firecrackers. A military officer living just across the street from the MCC house had been assassinated.

Later that same week Ron received a call from Jorge, a local MCC partner coordinating work in the greater San Salvador region. The guerrillas had overtaken one of the small villages and driven off the local military presence. It was the same village the three of us were planning to visit that day. We met at Jorge's house to decide if we should go. "We've seen this before," said Ron. "The guerrillas come in at night, take over the town, get food and supplies, and leave. Out of frustration the military will call for an air strike, but the people in the village are the ones who suffer. The guerrillas are long gone by the time the planes come." Ron was in the same village when one such air strike was launched. "I hid out in the MCC grain warehouse and prayed a bullet or bomb wouldn't land on me." So, do we go or not? "Jorge and I are planning to go. You have to decide if you want to stay here or ride along," they told me. At that moment I remembered a dream I had the night before I left for the airport. I was visiting my parents in Ohio and had been reading background material about the civil war and chilling stories of people who were "disappeared." As I fell asleep I had a vision of a bright light and a figure standing in the middle of it. I knew it was Jesus. A voice said, "Not yet, my son, not yet." I woke up the next morning, recorded the dream in my journal, and went to the airport. I had forgotten about it until that moment in Jorge's living room. I said, "If you two brothers of mine are going, I will too." It was a calculated risk, but I went with a real sense of calm and peace that God was watching over us. Nothing happened that day as we visited MCC workers who were assisting refugees near the village. Ron showed me the warehouse that had been strafed by military planes during the last retaliatory strike. He showed me where he had been arrested, handcuffed, and led to an interrogation room. I walked the path with him, trying to imagine the fear and uncertainty he must have felt that day. After a few hours of questioning Ron was released unharmed.

"'Be still, and know that I am God! I am exalted among the nations, I am exalted in the earth.' The Lord of hosts is with us; the God of Jacob is our refuge "(46:10-11). My brief time in Central America gave me a glimpse of Christians who believe God's promises of protection. There were very real risks to life and limb during that volatile time of conflict and war. Many brothers and sisters in Christ in Central America lost their lives. But they pledged their allegiance to the lamb who was slain and took God at his word. Singer Ray Boltz[5] writes:

Chorus:
I pledge allegiance to the Lamb
With all my strength
With all I am
I will seek to honor his commands
I pledge allegiance to the Lamb.

I have heard how Christians long ago
Were brought before a tyrant's throne
They were told that he would spare their lives
If they would renounce the name of Christ
But one by one they chose to die
The Son of God they would not deny
Like a great angelic choir sings
I can almost hear their voices ring.

Now the years have come and the years have gone
And the cause of Jesus still goes on
Now our time has come to count the cost
To reject the world, to embrace the cross
And one by one let us live our lives
For the One who died to give us life
Till the trumpet sounds on the final day
Let us proudly stand and boldly say

To the Lamb of God who bore my pain
Who took my place who wore my shame
I will seek to honor his commands
I pledge allegiance to the Lamb

When we confess Jesus as Lord and promise to follow Christ in life, we do so in the knowledge and expectation that the world may reject us the way Jesus was rejected. When we pledge our allegiance to the lamb we do so in the knowledge that the lamb we follow was slain and put to death on the cross. But we also know that the same lamb was triumphant in overcoming the forces of evil that put him on the cross in the first place. The resurrection makes all the difference in this equation. The calculated risks that MCC workers in Central America take are done so in the context of resurrection hope. Otherwise they are risks many would deem foolish. Risking to go where Jesus went, risking life and limb in the name of Christ, is a calculated risk that reflects the best of radical Christianity. So is protesting the death penalty, resisting the payment of war taxes, and joining a Christian Peacemaker Team. We believe that God saves us from our enemies, by his grace, the same way God saves us from our sins. And so we take what we sing, what we pray, and what we believe seriously. It's a matter of life and resurrection.

Questions for Discussion

1. What has been your experience with the Pledge of Allegiance or National Anthem? (Note: this is a different kind of discussion for Canadians and will need to be adapted accordingly.)
2. What other hymns come to mind that contain challenging words? Are we aware of their meaning?
3. Is it unrealistic to believe that God saves us from our enemies? Does our understanding of salvation include this dimension of God's work in our lives?
4. What experiences of "calculated risks" have you or members of the group had? How did your faith affect your decision?
5. Review Ray Boltz's alternative pledge. Do these words express your faith and belief?
6. Can we claim the song of Zechariah in Luke 1:68f. as our own? Is this paradox or prophecy?

9
Letting God Be the Judge

*We place our hope in the reign of God and in its
fulfillment in the day when Christ our ascended
Lord will come again in glory to judge the living
and the dead.*

—Article 24 in the *Confession of Faith
in a Mennonite Perspective*[1]

Key Texts *John 3:16*
"For God so loved the world that he gave his only Son, so
that everyone who believes in him may not perish but may
have eternal life."

Romans 12:19
Beloved, never avenge yourselves, but leave room for the
wrath of God; for it is written, "Vengeance is mine, I will
repay, says the Lord."

John 3:16 was the first Scripture verse I ever committed to
memory as a child. I don't recall now if it was in Sunday
school or Bible school but John 3:16 was the verse to learn.
I've heard sermons about the love of God for the whole world
used to support both Christian missions and stewardship of
natural resources. Believing and accepting Jesus as Savior and
Lord is the major thrust of evangelism and outreach. The part
about "perishing" conjures up images of hellfire and brim-
stone for all who don't believe. There is a lot at stake in this
one verse!

Croatian theologian Mirislov Volf makes this observation:

The Anabaptist tradition, consistently the most pacifist tradition
in the history of the Christian church, has traditionally had no
hesitation about speaking of God's wrath and judgment.[2]

The 1995 *Confession of Faith in a Mennonite Perspective* reflects this most clearly in Article 24, "The Reign of God." The word "judge" or "judgment" is used three times in this short article. An insightful word of explanation is found in the commentary.

> For some, the idea of God's final judgment is problematic, because it seems to emphasize God's wrath at the expense of God's love and mercy. God's loving patience is so great that God will not coerce anyone into covenant relationship, but will allow those who reject it to remain separated from God. Moreover, God's justice means that unrepentant evildoers will not go unpunished. Those who are suffering for righteousness' sake can look forward to the coming reign of God as a time of vindication and rescue from evil (Ps. 37; Rev. 6:9-11). In the age to come, there will be surprising reversals as the powerful are brought down and the lowly lifted up (Luke 1:52-53; see also Luke 3:5).[3]

As people of faith who have decided to pick up the cross of Christ and thus have disarmed their lives from violence and vengeance, this affirmation that God is the final arbiter over good and evil gives us hope and strength. Without it we would scarcely find the courage to risk life and limb for the sake of the kingdom. In the Old Testament we find two references to God's claim on vengeance. The first is Leviticus 19:18: "You shall not take vengeance or bear a grudge against any of your people, but you shall love your neighbor as yourself: I am the LORD." At first we might be tempted to see this only as an injunction against fellow believers or those in our immediate community or neighborhood. Jesus, however, broadens the definition of neighbor in the familiar story of the compassionate Samaritan (Luke 10). No longer could the parameters of compassion be extended to only those we love and like.

The second Old Testament reference is found in Deuteronomy 32:35-36, "Vengeance is mine, and recompense, for the time when their foot shall slip; because the day of their calamity is at hand, their doom comes swiftly. Indeed the LORD will vindicate his people, have compassion on his servants, when he sees that their power is gone, neither bond nor free remaining." Both Paul and the writer of Hebrews draw upon these texts in their admonition to fellow believers. Paul writes to the church in Rome, "Beloved, never avenge yourselves, but leave room for the wrath of God; for it is written, 'Vengeance is mine, I will repay,' says the Lord" (Rom. 12:19).

The message is twofold: we are not to avenge ourselves in the short run, and God will make things right in the long run. In Hebrews the emphasis is a little different (10:30-31): "For we know the one who said, 'Vengeance is mine, I will repay.' And again, 'The Lord will judge his people.' It is a fearful thing to fall into the hands of the living God." The Puritan preacher Jonathan Edwards may have had this text in mind when he thundered from the pulpit that we are merely "Sinners in the hands of an angry God." While we acknowledge God as righteous judge of all humanity, we also embrace the same God who is "slow to anger abounding in steadfast love" (Ps. 103:8). The second commandment teaches why we are not to fashion anything that detracts or takes away our devotion from God.

> You shall not make for yourself an idol, whether in the form of anything that is in heaven above, or that is on the earth beneath, or that is in the water under the earth. You shall not bow down to them or worship them; for I the LORD your God am a jealous God, punishing children for the iniquity of parents, to the third and the fourth generation of those who reject me, but showing steadfast love to the thousandth generation of those who love me and keep my commandments (Exod. 20:4-6).

Notice how the judgment of God is delimited to one multigenerational household. By contrast, God's steadfast love is endless. The emphasis is on God's nature and preference for love toward those who would worship God and live in obedience to God's way for the world. This does not negate the jealous nature of God when it comes to idolatry, it simply puts it into perspective. The question is, have we made self-preservation at all costs an idol in our culture? Does the worship of self lead to the attitude that I must protect myself and prolong my life on this earth as long as possible? Idolatry takes many forms—from consumerism and an obsession with wealth to protecting our possessions and investments. The doctrine of self-preservation may be another form of idolatry.

Letting God be the judge also means respecting what God has created in God's own image. If we believe that every human being is made in the image of God (Gen. 1) and God sent Jesus into the world because he loved the *whole* world (John 3:16), then people of faith cannot act as the ultimate judge, jury, and executioner of another human being. To do so is to potentially deny that other person the chance to be reconciled with God. Human free will argues for the possibility that some will forever choose not to be in fellowship with God. But in the final judgment we are not the ones making the decision. John Howard Yoder points out that when we use lethal violence to defend the life of a loved one who is a person of faith we reverse the fundamental belief that God is the judge of people's ultimate destiny—both the loved one and the aggressor. "To keep out of heaven temporarily someone who wants to go there ultimately anyway, I would consign to hell immediately someone whom I am in the world to save."[4]

For some Christians it is a radical leap of faith to embrace the practical implications of loving their enemy. So what about killing fellow believers? If Christians hold the position that they should obey the governing authorities (Rom. 13) including the call to arms, then theoretically it is possible for Christians in two opposing nations to find themselves prepared to kill each other. Squared off in combat or more likely behind the controls of a guided missile or "smart bomb," people who confess Jesus as Lord, yet pledge allegiance to their flag, are prepared to take the life of a brother or sister in Christ. Does that make sense? John Stoner's poster gained in-

ternational attention because it was so obvious in its truthful-
ness: *A Modest Proposal for Peace: Let the Christians of the
world agree that they will not kill each other.* The Anabaptist
contribution to the church-state dilemma is that the Christian
cannot operate in both realms under two distinct sets of rules,
one for the church and one for the state. Rather, the gospel
compels us to follow Christ in all of life and to live by a consistent ethic of love and nonviolence. No wonder the six-
teenth-century Anabaptists were called Radicals.[5]

Using the cross as a sword. In a Catholic cemetery in Belfast,
Northern Ireland, is a memorial to those who died in World
War II. At first I was struck by the irony of a cross used for a
war memorial. But as I got closer I noticed something even
more disturbing. Superimposed on the cross, running the
length and breadth of this giant cross, was a sword. I had
never thought of the similarity in quite that way. On the other
hand, who wouldn't want God on their side going into battle?
Once Christians make the decision to pick up the sword they
tend to shape their doctrine around their actions. From holy
war to just war, Christians from the time of Constantine have
found a way to overlay the cross with the sword, to self-ap-
point themselves to be the harbingers of God's judgment on
earth. To me this seems blasphemous and contrary to what we
have just read in Scripture. Is it not time to disarm the cross?
Can we let the power of God and the promise of resurrection
bring the sword down from the cross? Is the cross not alone
powerful enough to save us?

Trusting God. When Christians pick up the sword to defend
themselves or their loved ones it would be natural to call upon
God for protection. But where do we get the idea that God's
will for our lives is one of self-preservation? Jesus said, "If any
want to become my followers, let them deny themselves and
take up their cross daily and follow me" (Luke 9:23). He never
said "If any want to become my followers, let them defend

themselves and take up their sword daily and follow me." Following Christ daily means the crucifixion of our presumption of self-preservation and the radical reliance on God's protection. Volf sums it up this way:

> Without entrusting oneself to the God who judges justly, it will hardly be possible to follow the crucified Messiah and refuse to retaliate when abused. The certainty of God's just judgment at the end of history is the presupposition for the renunciation of violence in the middle of it.[6]

Our faith and radical trust in God means we allow God to be the judge of another human being, not us. We renounce violence in any form from self-defense, abortion, domestic violence, the death penalty, and war.[7] We are consistently pro-life. But can we trust that God's judgment will be consistent with God's love of the whole world and everyone in it? If God demonstrates sacrificial love for sinners on the cross, how much more will God demonstrate this love at the end of time?[8] That part is unknown to us. In the meantime, we are called to disarm the cross, pick it up to follow Jesus, and trust that God will take care of the rest.

Questions for Discussion

1. What has been your understanding of John 3:16?
2. How does God's judgment inform your faith and non-violence?
3. How do we hold in balance the loving character of God and God as eternal judge? Do we assume that God's judgment at the end of time is necessarily violent?
4. Is belief in self-preservation at all costs a form of idolatry? Elaborate.
5. Review John Stoner's "A Modest Proposal for Peace." What implications does this have for us as people of faith?
6. Think of other examples of how the sword and the cross get connected. How can we help disarm the cross?

10
The Cross and Evil

Strike against war, for without you no battles can be fought! Strike against manufacturing shrapnel and gas bombs and all other tools of murder! Strike against preparedness that means death and misery to millions of human beings! Be not dumb, obedient slaves in an army of destruction! Be heroes in an army of construction!

—Helen Keller[1]

Key Text *Romans 12:9-21*

Let love be genuine; hate what is evil, hold fast to what is good; love one another with mutual affection; outdo one another in showing honor. Do not lag in zeal, be ardent in spirit, serve the Lord. Rejoice in hope, be patient in suffering, persevere in prayer. Contribute to the needs of the saints; extend hospitality to strangers. Bless those who persecute you; bless and do not curse them. Rejoice with those who rejoice, weep with those who weep. Live in harmony with one another; do not be haughty, but associate with the lowly; do not claim to be wiser than you are. Do not repay anyone evil for evil, but take thought for what is noble in the sight of all. If it is possible, so far as it depends on you, live peaceably with all. Beloved, never avenge yourselves, but leave room for the wrath of God; for it is written, "Vengeance is mine, I will repay, says the Lord." No, "if your enemies are hungry, feed them; if they are thirsty, give them something to drink; for by doing this you will heap burning coals on their heads." Do not be overcome by evil, but overcome evil with good.

One of the earliest memories I have growing up on the farm was when we would slaughter a chicken. Mom and Dad would hang the chicken on the clothesline and cut off its head. One time a chicken wriggled free from the line and began running around the yard, blood spurting from its severed neck. It was a literal portrayal of that proverbial phrase of someone running around "like a chicken with its head cut off." As a child it was all too graphic and frightening. My mind told me that chicken was already dead or at least dying. My emotions told me to run like crazy!

Vernard Eller refers to a similarly primitive scene as a way of describing the manifestation of evil between the cross and the kingdom.

> Far from becoming anxious and frustrated over the seeming intransigence of the industrial-military complex and the apparent impossibility of making any perceptible dent upon the world, the Christian peacemaker knows that the monster already has been decapitated by the sharp two-edged sword of Jesus.[2]

The book of Daniel breathes an air of confidence that God is triumphing over worldly powers of evil. Do we share that confidence and act on that faith? Jesus on the cross conquered evil and death. Satan and his power is already overcome by the love of God and the sacrifice of Jesus Christ on the cross. We know that, confess that, and claim that promise. However, we live in the "already and not yet" time between the reality of the cross and the time when the kingdom of God will come in its fullness. God's reign is not yet recognized by the world and evil is still on the loose. Though decapitated, the monster is still running wild. We know how the story will end, but in the meantime it is quite frightening. Somehow we have to come to grips as people of faith with this dual reality. On the one hand we believe that nothing can separate us from the love of God in Christ Jesus (Rom. 8:35-39). On the other hand we know that bad things still happen to good people, that evil seems to have its way in war, genocide, murder, and mayhem. How do Christians live in such a time as this? What should our approach be to evil in the real world?

In the book of Romans, Chapter 12, Paul makes four references to evil. In verse 9 he says boldly, "Hate what is evil." Those are strong words, words that seem contradictory to our commandment to love as God loves. But evil is and has always been, at cross-purposes with God. Evil is what separates us from God, interferes with our obedience to God's intentions for our lives, and contradicts our faith in "the more excellent way" (1 Cor. 13). That we should hate what is evil is no surprise; how that hatred translates into action on the other hand, is surprising.

Verse 17 takes this Christian resistance to evil to the next level. "Do not repay evil for evil." That is our first clue to the alternative way of Jesus and our approach to evil. Do not fight fire with fire. Do not employ the currency of evil. Not fighting evil with evil is a ministry of restraint. It means that we refuse to let others' actions determine our own. It means that we will not stoop down to the level of evil to resist evil. Not repaying evil for evil expresses our commitment to keep our means and ends compatible and will be discussed in the next chapter. We cannot justify the end result if how we get there violates the very principles we stand for. Catholic peacemaker Richard McSorely argues that "the gospel teaches us that there is an integral relationship between the goal that God sets for us in life, the destiny that he has for us, and the means that we use to get to it."[3] Where we are headed makes all the difference in how we get there. McSorely continues:

> The destiny that God sets for us, as Thomas Merton puts it, is to participate in the divine life, to know ourselves as children of God and to grow in that knowledge. And the means to accomplish that participation are to feed the hungry, clothe the naked, give shelter to the homeless, and bear one another's burdens in this pilgrimage of life. So the means are compatible with—in agreement with—the end, and they are even reversible with the end. That's all clear and simple gospel. And yet it's completely opposite to the nature of militarism and to what's taught in every political science and government course that I've ever heard of. What's taught is, *Through strength we get peace.*

Which means, *Through war, through killing, we get peace. Through dishonor we get honor. Through lying and deceit we get morality. Through chaos we get good order. Through rape and arson and destruction and mayhem we get a better world. Through destroying we get creation.* That's the process of war. It's on a sign on the grounds of the Air Force Academy in Colorado Springs, Colorado. It says, "Peace is our profession." There, it's all very simple. And the means to the peace? Everything the air force uses: nuclear bombs, other kinds of bombs, cannons, machine guns. Out of a bad tree you don't get good fruit. Out of an evil means you don't get a good result.[4]

The couplet in verse 21 completes Paul's teaching on evil in Romans 12. "Do not be overcome by evil, but overcome evil with good." Not being overcome by evil is perhaps the hardest part of this teaching. If we are to hate what is evil we want to do something about it. We want to act on that hate. But if we are not to employ evil means to achieve good ends, and if we are not to be overcome by evil, how do we do it? The military imagery of Ephesians 6 is instructive here.

Finally, be strong in the Lord and in the strength of his power. Put on the whole armor of God, so that you may be able to stand against the wiles of the devil. For our struggle is not against enemies of blood and flesh, but against the rulers, against the authorities, against the cosmic powers of this present darkness, against the spiritual forces of evil in the heavenly places. Therefore take up the whole armor of God, so that you may be able to withstand on that evil day, and having done everything, to stand firm. Stand therefore, and fasten the belt of truth around your waist, and put on the breastplate of righteousness. As shoes for your feet put on whatever will make you ready to proclaim the gospel of peace. With all of these, take the shield of faith, with which you will be able to quench all the flaming arrows of the evil one. Take the helmet of salvation, and the sword of the Spirit, which is the word of God (Eph. 6:10-17).

Vernard Eller points out that this armor of God is for *defensive* purposes.[5] People are not the enemy. The principalities

and powers are God's enemies and our role is to wrap ourselves with the armor God provides for us to defend ourselves
against evil: the belt of truth, the breastplate of righteousness,
the helmet of salvation, the sword of the Spirit, and the shoes
of peace. Overcoming evil with good is what we find in Jesus.
His teachings tell us to fight fire with water, to return good for
evil, to pray for our persecutors, to love our enemies, to give
them food and water, to kill their evil intentions with kindness.
In all of our favorite stories from classic Westerns to Star Wars
we want good to triumph over evil. But we are too easily se-
duced into believing that the one with the bigger gun or light
saber always wins. The biblical way of good triumphing over
evil is to appear to lose. The hero of our story is a lamb that
was slain. Jesus is not a lion or a bear or a shark. He's a lamb,
a sacrificial lamb. But this lamb is the one who triumphs, who
is worthy to open the scrolls at the end of time and unleash
the goodness of God's kingdom "on earth as it is in heaven."

There is a cosmic battle that rages and it is naive to think
that good people, innocent people, people of faith, are immune from it. We are not immune from the destructive forces
that are unleashed when people do evil things. Sometimes
there are senseless and meaningless acts of destruction and
death and we are forever affected by it. But we are not de-
feated. We are not overcome. We are not sucked into the destructive spiral of violence that seeks revenge, that seeks retribution, that imposes more pain and suffering on the perpetra-
tor and calls it justice. Our way is a different way. Our way is
the way of God and Jesus. Our way challenges the dominant
culture of redemptive violence. Our way declares that faith
and love and forgiveness and reconciliation have so transformed our lives that nothing can separate us from the love of
God. And because we are *always* safe and secure in that love
we will stand ready, without fear, to die for our faith. But we
will not kill for our faith. We will not barter with the currency of evil and we will not try to overcome evil with greater
evil. Theologian John Stott sums it up this way,

In all our thinking and living it is important to keep the negative and positive counterparts together. Both are good. It is good never to retaliate, because if we repay evil for evil, we double it, adding a second evil to the first, and so increasing the tally of evil in the world. It is even better to be positive, to bless, to do good, to seek peace, and to serve and convert our enemy, because if we thus repay good for evil, we reduce the tally of evil in the world, while at the same time increasing the tally of good. To repay evil for evil is to be overcome by it; to repay good for evil is to overcome evil with good. This is the way of the cross.[6]

By seeing the macro view of how God approaches evil in Jesus Christ, we gain perspective on how we as followers of Jesus Christ approach evil on the micro level. Remember Paul's words in Romans 12:18, "If it is possible, so far as it depends on *you*, live peaceably with all" (emphasis mine). Taking our cues from Scripture and the community of faith puts us at odds with the dominant culture, if not most of the world. But is that not the calling of our "narrow way"? Are we so concerned about fitting in with the world that we are ill-fitted for the whole armor of God? Evil, in all its various manifestations, may give us pause and seriously challenge our faith. The next two chapters expand further the example that Jesus gives us in resisting oppression, loving our enemies, and overcoming evil with good. While the headless chicken of evil may frighten us in the short run, we know that its fate is already determined and that we shall not be overcome in the long run.

Questions for Discussion

1. Think of other examples of how we live between the "already and the not yet" of God's kingdom.
2. How have Christians over the centuries responded to evil? Are there examples from your own tradition or church that help focus this challenge?
3. The Ephesians 6 passage often gets "spiritualized" to only apply to spiritual warfare. Do you believe that it

also applies to the question of self-preservation? What is it that we most seek to preserve?

4. How does the dominant culture send messages that violence can be redemptive?

5. Read again the quote from John Stott. Discuss his reasoning of reducing the tally of evil in the world while increasing the tally of good. What are other examples of this equation?

11
Christ's Third Way

Human evolution has provided the species with two deeply instinctual responses to violence: flight or fight. Jesus offers a third way: nonviolent direct action.

—Walter Wink[1]

Key Text *Matthew 5:38-45*

"You have heard that it was said, 'An eye for an eye and a tooth for a tooth.' But I say to you, Do not resist an evildoer. But if anyone strikes you on the right cheek, turn the other also; and if anyone wants to sue you and take your coat, give your cloak as well; and if anyone forces you to go one mile, go also the second mile. Give to everyone who begs from you, and do not refuse anyone who wants to borrow from you. "You have heard that it was said, 'You shall love your neighbor and hate your enemy.' But I say to you, Love your enemies and pray for those who persecute you, so that you may be children of your Father in heaven; for he makes his sun rise on the evil and on the good, and sends rain on the righteous and on the unrighteous.

Mark B. hated my guts. He was a year older, a little bigger, and a lot meaner. When his girlfriend Connie broke up with him, he blamed ME! I know now that this was inappropriate and displaced anger over a situation he felt helpless to rectify. But at the time, all I knew is that I should stay out of Mark's way, at least as long as Connie and I were going steady. That summer we worked on the same truck-farm crew and he kept throwing dirt clods at me. Luckily his aim was off and I was really good at dodging things since I grew up on a farm with three brothers.

Then one day at our local swimming hole (complete with beach sand) Mark came up to me and literally kicked sand at me. I knew this was showdown time. I figured I had three options: One, run like a crazy man and get out of there as fast as I could (flight). I was pretty quick and could likely make it to my car. Two, take him on like I would my older brother (fight). Mark wasn't near the size of my older brother Dan who weighed in at 200 pounds and was the starting center for the varsity footfall team. Or three, try and talk him out of it (third way). Couldn't we just act civilized and work this out? My fears told me to run. My pride told me to fight. My spirit told me to talk him out of it. What should I do?

In the Sermon on the Mount, Jesus challenges us with a third way to respond to violence. "An eye for an eye, tooth for a tooth" is one of the oldest laws on the books. It is found in the *Code of Hammurabi* which dates back to the 17th century B.C. *Lex Talionis* literally means "law of retaliation." The intent was to limit the retaliation a person could inflict on the one who was at fault. So if someone breaks your arm you can't break both their arms and their legs. The most you can do under the law is break one arm. If they poke your eye out accidentally, you can't legally poke both the other person's eyes out in revenge. Building on the Code of Hammurabi, the Mosaic Law says: "Anyone who maims another shall suffer the same injury in return: fracture for fracture, eye for eye, tooth for tooth; the injury inflicted is the injury to be suffered" (Lev. 24:19-20). "Show no pity: life for life, eye for eye, tooth for tooth, hand for hand, foot for foot" (Deut. 19:21).

Our criminal justice system still operates largely on this retribution system. The courts try to make the punishment fit the crime. In extreme cases, if you take someone's life you are given the death penalty, a life for a life. Violence is prone to escalate, each side taking revenge on the other for the previous injury. Gandhi said, "An eye for an eye only ends up making the whole world blind."[2]

But then Jesus came along and said, "Love your enemies and pray for those who persecute you" (Matt. 5:44). Already he's gotten the attention of his listeners. He's either been in the sun too long or has a new angle on a very old problem. He then gives some concrete examples: turn the other cheek, give them your cloak, go the second mile. These texts are familiar enough to have been tamed by the accepted interpretation: take undeserved punishment, be generous in adversity, and sacrificially go the distance. *Lex Talionis* calls for an equal measure of revenge, so Jesus must be talking about nonresistance; "Let them hit me, let them sue me, I'll trudge the extra mile for my Lord." But maybe there is another way to look at what Jesus is teaching.

The listeners are those being victimized. Notice that Jesus said, "When someone strikes *you* on the right cheek. . . . When someone sues *you* for your cloak. . . . When someone forces *you* to go one mile. . . ." He isn't talking to the perpetrators, but the folks on the receiving end. That's an important distinction. He didn't say: "When you hit someone go easy on them. When you sue someone only ask for the minimum." Or, "When you exercise your right and force someone to carry your pack don't push 'em too hard." No, these are the victims he's addressing. So what is Jesus telling the victimized?

If someone strikes you on the right cheek. First-century Palestine was a right-handed world. The right hand was the hand of power and strength, the right side the place of honor and protection. The left hand was considered deceitful and deadly.

(Judg. 3:21) Then Ehud reached with his *left hand*, took the sword from his right thigh, and thrust it into Eglon's belly (*emphasis mine*).

(Judg. 20:16) Of all this force, there were seven hundred picked men who were left-handed; every one could sling a stone at a hair, and not miss.

(2 Sam. 20:9-10) Joab said to Amasa, "Is it well with you, my brother?" And Joab took Amasa by the beard with his *right hand* to kiss him. But Amasa did not notice the sword in Joab's (left) hand; Joab struck him in the belly so that his entrails poured out on the ground, and he died. He did not strike a second blow. Then Joab and his brother Abishai pursued Sheba son of Bichri. (*insertion mine*)

The Dead Sea Scrolls contained a law from the Qumran community of the Essenes, extreme isolationists who thought it virtuous to hate the sinner. "One who brings out his left hand to (make a gesture) with it shall be punished ten days."[3] Since Jesus specified the right cheek, the only way to logically hit someone in a civilized society is with the back of the right hand. So what? This was not uncommon for a master to hit a slave or for someone in a prominent position to punish or insult or admonish a subordinate or lower class person. But it was a major offense if you inflicted it upon a peer. Jewish oral tradition says:

> If one cuffs his fellow, he must pay him a *sela*. Rabbi Judah, in the name of Rabbi Jose the Galilean, says, A *maneh*. If he slapped him he must pay him two hundred *zuz*; [if he hit him] with the back of his hand, he must pay him four hundred *zuz* . . . . This is the general principle: it all depends on a person's dignity.[4]

If you are poor, a slave, a Gentile, a Samaritan, a tax collector, or a disabled person, you don't have much honor. So when Jesus says, "Turn the other cheek," he is saying, "Now the person insulting you must hit you with his open palm," a slap that would most likely be given to a peer. You don't hit back or insult back. You are even ready to take the physical pain of the insult. But you stand your ground and challenge the injustice of the person who is insulting you, *as if you are an equal*. That is not passive nonresistance but active nonviolence.

If anyone wants to sue you and take your coat, give your cloak as well. By Jewish law if you are so in debt that you can't pay, or if you borrowed something of value from someone, your cloak, used as a coat for protection and warmth but also for your blanket at night, was given as collateral. Because of this double usage it had to be given back by sundown (Exod. 22:26). Your tunic on the other hand was the garment worn next to your skin, your shirt. "Give them the shirt off your back" probably comes from this verse. So what is Jesus saying? It appears to be, if rich creditors push to the point where they are suing you for your clothes, *go all the way*. The economic system was so bad and people so poor that Jesus says expose it—literally! Clown a little bit. Offer him your tunic as well and parade around bareback. The shame when someone is naked was not on the one without clothes, but on those who see him without clothes. Take the example of Noah's sons:

> Noah, a man of the soil, was the first to plant a vineyard. He drank some of the wine and became drunk, and he lay uncovered in his tent. And Ham, the father of Canaan, saw the nakedness of his father, and told his two brothers outside. Then Shem and Japheth took a garment, laid it on both their shoulders, and walked backward and covered the nakedness of their father; their faces were turned away, and they did not see their father's nakedness (Gen. 9:20-23).

The Jewish Talmud had this to offer, "If your neighbor calls you an ass, put a saddle on your back."[5] Clowning, playing out the logic of an illogical situation was Jesus' suggestion. Neither fight nor flight.

If someone forces you to go one mile go two. Palestine was occupied territory. The Roman legions and their entourages were always passing through or rotating their troops. There were mile markers on the roads and a soldier could legally impress a civilian to let him borrow his donkey or make him carry his pack (weighing up to 60 pounds). But *only for one mile* so as not to anger or incite the local population. So what is Jesus saying? Go the extra mile and see what happens. Will the soldier get in trouble? What will he think you're up to when you don't do the expected? Can you see this legionnaire looking over his shoulder, wondering if his commander is watching, hoping he doesn't get caught abusing one of the locals? Take control of the situation, change the equation between the powerful and powerless, level the playing field.

But what about the words "do not resist"? The Greek word *anthistemi* is a translation challenge. Most translations use "do not resist" and thus the term *nonresistance*. But two translations come closer to the intended meaning according to Walter Wink. *The New English Bible* says, "Do not set yourself against the man who wrongs you." *Today's English Version* renders it, "Do not take revenge on someone who wrongs you." Wink points out the consistency of this translation with Paul's words in Romans 12:

> Do not repay anyone evil for evil, but take thought for what is noble in the sight of all. If it is possible, so far as it depends on you, live peaceably with all. Beloved, never avenge yourselves, but leave room for the wrath of God; for it is written, "Vengeance is mine, I will repay, says the Lord" (Rom. 12:17-19).

Not taking revenge or employing the currency of tit-for-tat violence, that's the key to understanding Jesus' third way. But refusing to take revenge is not the same as doing nothing or taking flight. Nonresistance is too often equated with passiveness, inaction, or silent suffering. *Active nonviolence* is more accurate to describe the third way of Jesus.

In the Sermon on the Mount, Jesus teaches us that retributive justice and revenge is not the answer, but neither is passive inaction. Turn the other cheek and claim your humanity. Be bold enough to act the clown when the occasion calls for it. Go the extra mile and challenge the oppressive system. Wink is careful to point out that these teachings are *examples* that must be contextualized and applied. But the emphasis is on creative, nonviolent, direct action. There is in fact an Old Testament precedent to this way of thinking. When the Jews many centuries ago were asked to worship Caesar, their defiance could have led to war. Here's what they did:

> They replied, "We will not by any means make war with him, but still we will die before we see our laws transgressed." So they threw themselves down upon their faces, and stretched out their throats, and said they were ready to be slain; and this they did for forty days together, and in the mean time left of the tilling of their ground, and that while the season of the year required them to sow it. Thus they continued firm in their resolution, and proposed to themselves to die willingly, rather than to see the dedication of the statue.[6]

Today, creative nonviolence is being employed by Christian Peacemaker Teams in situations of conflict around the world.[7] Imagine what would happen if all the Christians of the world joined CPT instead of the military?

When Mark B. kicked sand on me at the beach I knew it was a moment of truth. Do I clench my fist and give him what he deserved for all his harassment? Do I run away and break up with Connie and end this hassle? I took the third option. I stood up and looked him in the eye and said, "Mark, fighting isn't going to solve anything." I calmly walked away and turned my back to him. He called me a few names and cursed at me, but I felt like it was the right thing to do. Nothing more happened for which I am thankful. Besides, he ended up marrying Connie anyway! As Christians who take seriously the words of Jesus we are challenged by the examples in the Sermon on the Mount to choose neither fight nor flight. There is another way, the way of nonviolent direct action, the way of Jesus.

Questions for Discussion:

1. Have you ever been confronted with a situation that called for a creative non-violent response?
2. Is non-violent direct action consistent with your understanding of nonresistance?
3. Does Wink's interpretation of the Sermon on the Mount ring true. If not, why not?
4. Read or download the Christian Peacemaker Team Website information. Does your church currently support the work of CPT?
5. How does this chapter challenge your assumptions about fight or flight?
6. For further reading see *Mennonite Peacemaking: from Quietism to Activism* by Leo Driedger and Donald B. Kraybill. Scottdale: Herald Press, 1994.

12
What Would Jesus Do?

"It's not the dying that I was afraid of. It was the killing."

—Dink Jenkins[1]

Key Texts *John 12:24*
Very truly, I tell you, unless a grain of wheat falls into the earth and dies, it remains just a single grain; but if it dies, it bears much fruit.

John 18:36
Jesus answered, "My kingdom is not from this world. If my kingdom were from this world, my followers would be fighting to keep me from being handed over to the Jews. But as it is, my kingdom is not from here."

1 Peter 2:20-24
If you endure when you are beaten for doing wrong, what credit is that? But if you endure when you do right and suffer for it, you have God's approval. For to this you have been called, because Christ also suffered for you, leaving you an example, so that you should follow in his steps. "He committed no sin, and no deceit was found in his mouth." When he was abused, he did not return abuse; when he suffered, he did not threaten; but he entrusted himself to the one who judges justly. He himself bore our sins in his body on the cross, so that, free from sins, we might live for righteousness; by his wounds you have been healed.

In His Steps by Charles Sheldon was a best-selling book.[2] It told the somewhat idealized story of a pastor who decided to face every decision in his life by asking, "What would Jesus do?" This motto became popularized in the late 1990s when a youth leader decided it would be a good reminder to her youth. WWJD bracelets, bumper stickers, and T-shirts were the result. But did people really get the message? Are we really prepared to do what Jesus did?

A better starting point is to ask, "What did Jesus do?" How did Jesus face the challenges of self-preservation and what can we learn from his example? "In his steps" is a phrase from 1 Peter 2:21. But did you notice what the example of Jesus was for us? It is suffering. Suffering is something that most of the time we make every effort to avoid. Who among us *chooses* to suffer? In the Anabaptist-Mennonite tradition we point to the *Martyrs Mirror* as evidence of a suffering faith. The Anabaptists were willing to suffer for their convictions. Are we? A replica tongue screw[3] sits on my office desk, a gruesome reminder of how desperate the authorities were to silence the voices of Anabaptists being led to their execution. As we mentioned in chapter two, the New Testament Greek word for *witness* became synonymous with *martyr* as the early church fell under persecution. Jesus' words to the disciples take on new urgency when we substitute martyr for witness. "But you will receive power when the Holy Spirit has come upon you; and you will be my witnesses [martyrs] in Jerusalem, in all Judea and Samaria, and to the ends of the earth" (Acts 1:8). Witnessing is more than a verbal expression of our faith. It is also how we live out our lives in the name of Jesus by the power of the Holy Spirit. And that includes how we face threats to our personal safety.

Cassie Bernall said, "Yes," when Eric Harris pointed a gun at the Columbine High School student's head and asked, "Do you believe in God?" According to witnesses, as he pulled the trigger, he further tormented by asking, "Why?" Cassie couldn't answer. She lay dying with a bullet in her head. Cassie Bernall, though whether or not she was the one who said, "Yes," has since been challenged, has become a Christian martyr since the fatal shootings in Colorado in April of 1999. But there is an interesting twist to Cassie's story that her mother relates in her book *She Said Yes: The Unlikely Martyrdom of Cassie Bernall*.[4] A writer for the *Chicago Tribune*, in reviewing the book, comments that the strength of the story is that Cassie was a normal, troubled teenager who wasn't looking to be a hero.

> Unlike the martyr narratives that shaped early Christianity, Cassie is not endowed with supernatural insight or given miraculous visions. Nor are her parents. She is just a kid. And they are confused parents. Therein is the book's power. This is not a martyr's tale. It is a mourner's meditation—a mother's story of the death of a beloved and normal teenager. "Cassie is my daughter," writes Misty Bernall protectively. "You can't turn her into Joan of Arc."[5]

What I find instructive from Cassie's story is that when we get behind the sensationalism of a young woman professing her faith in the face of death, we find a real human being searching for an identity that includes faith. The newspaper writer goes on to point out that Plough Publishing, the publisher of *She Said Yes*, is an Anabaptist publishing house and that Anabaptist theology and piety is more about discipleship than the "accept Jesus and get born again" ethos of popular evangelicalism.

> "She Said Yes" is about discipleship, another term for the spiritual journey of saying yes to God. Cassie's yes was not a once-for-all. She had to keep saying it amid her troubles: Yes, yes, and yes. These yeses transformed but did not perfect her character. She was a girl in the process of becoming a better person through saying yes.[6]

When a person of faith dies it is by definition a bittersweet experience. As my pastor years ago said at the funeral of a young adult killed in a tragic auto accident "We grieve for what we feel, we rejoice for what we know."[7] Jesus captured this mix of loss and victory when he said, "Very truly, I tell you, unless a grain of wheat falls into the earth and dies, it remains just a single grain; but if it dies, it bears much fruit" (John 12:24). As our fears of death die within us because of our faith in Jesus, a new resurrection hope springs up to take its place. We do not go out looking for a premature end to our life, but neither do we go to extremes to avoid it. We struggle with the admiration we have of martyrs on the one hand and the fear of becoming one ourselves on the other. In that sense we are literally threatened by the idea of being resurrected!

Making sense of self-sacrifice. We have argued throughout this book that the choice of self-sacrifice makes sense given the parameters of our faith. Putting ourselves into situations of potential danger and possible harm is not rational if seen only through the lens of self-preservation. But when we trust the promises of God that resurrection awaits us at the end of our earthly life, and that we will experience the kingdom of God most fully when we go to join God and the company of all those who have gone before, then picking up our cross and following Jesus is logical. Rodney Stark, in his book *The Rise of Christianity*, points out that social scientists who study religion conclude that faith practices in general and martyrdom in particular are *irrational*. Trying to understand religious practice from outside the context of faith ends up discrediting more than understanding. Only recently has there been an attempt to understand the economics of faith-based choices focused on desired outcomes. In Stark's words:

> When analyzed properly, religious sacrifices and stigmas—even when acute cases are considered—usually turn out to represent rational choices. Indeed, the more that people must sacrifice for their faith, the greater the value of the rewards they gain in return. Put in conventional economic language, in terms of the ratio of costs to benefits, within limits the more expensive the religion, the better bargain it is.[8]

This is pivotal in our understanding of saying yes to Jesus and following Christ in life. "What would Jesus do?" is a question for a mature faith. In real terms the answer may well be at polar opposites of what my parents say, or my boss, or my classmates, or my government. When faced with threats to self or property, North American society says, "Arm yourself."[9] If attacked, fight back. If pushed, push back harder. If wronged, sue them for damages. If threatened, launch a preemptive strike. Media culture sends this message in countless ways—video games like "Mortal Combat" or movies such as "The Patriot" and "Gladiator"—where good conquers evil through a greater show of force. It is often subtle and sneaks up on our psyche. A job offer comes after college and the company with the defense contractor offers the best salary and benefits. An uncle did well as a highway state patrolman and there is an opening at the academy. A cousin got her tuition paid for by joining ROTC at the university. The investment portfolio our financial adviser presents includes stocks in the military-industrial complex and he points out that they've always outperformed the social choice options. The churchwide periodical reminds us yearly that nearly half of our tax dollars fund the cost of current and past military spending. Do we really want to take on the IRS and risk a penalty or an audit? So, does our faith still make sense to us when our job, education, and financial choices are directly affected, not to mention our personal security?

The other kingdom. When Pilate asks Jesus what he has done to get himself arrested, Jesus replies, "My kingdom is not from this world. If my kingdom were from this world, my followers would be fighting to keep me from being handed over to the Jews. But as it is, my kingdom is not from here" (John 18:36). A simple word study reveals that the New Testament has a lot more to say about God's kingdom than it does about heaven. Heaven tends to be associated with harps and clouds and angel wings, someplace "out there" that is totally other-worldly and more Hollywood than biblical. Kingdom language tells about a new world, a transformed social order that has broken people made whole, food enough for everyone, and a place in God's household. In the coming kingdom, death is absent and mourning and sorrow have turned to joy. So when Jesus tells Pilate that he and his disciples live day-to-day by the ethics of this other kingdom, fighting to prevent his arrest is not an option. If he was trying to establish an earthly kingdom and attempting to overthrow the Roman occupation troops, then an armed rebellion it would be. "But my kingdom is not of this world." Donald Kraybill's best-selling book *The Upside-Down Kingdom* popularized the idea of this alternative way of life. As Kraybill points out in his preface, this book is about taking "the New Testament and Jesus quite seriously."[10] Isn't that what the Christian life is supposed to be about, taking the Bible and Jesus seriously? So why is it so hard to take Jesus at his word (and example) when it comes to self-preservation? Because it is counter to the dominant culture and conventional wisdom.

Thy will be done. If we really want to be obedient to Jesus and do what he would do in any given situation, then we must submit our own wishes to those of God. In the Lord's Prayer Jesus prayed, "Thy will be done, on earth as it is in heaven." We live in the time between the cross and the coming of God's kingdom in its fullness. In the meantime, we try to create and reflect as best we can with our limited, human, and imperfect attempts, that coming kingdom—"on earth as it is in heaven." As a seminary classmate of mine once observed about radical Christians: "We believe what Jesus said, and we believe he meant it for us." Taking Jesus and the Bible seriously means living by upside-down kingdom ethics. It means choosing to live at odds with mainstream society. William Barclay sums up this challenge in his commentary on the Lord's Prayer:

The fact of life is quite simple. When the will of God insists that we face some difficult and sore and even agonizing situation, there is nothing to stop running away from it. Jesus could have turned back in Gethsemane. But, if we do run away from it, there can be no happiness in life, for there can be no happiness when a man [sic] cannot face either himself or God any longer. But if we do face it, with all it demands, then in life there is a peace and a joy and a satisfaction that nothing else can give. That is why Plato long ago said that the wise man will always prefer to suffer wrong rather than to do wrong, and that is why the whole lesson of Revelation is that there is all the difference in the world between *life* and *existence*, and that it may be that, if a man chooses to continue to *exist,* he may well forfeit *life.* To us the choice will not be between life and death, but it may be the choice between comfort and struggle, between ease and sacrifice; and it may well be that if we choose *pleasure*, we shall lose *joy*, for joy is the product of obedience to the will of God.[11]

Questions for Discussion

1. Read again 1 Peter 2:20-24 and discuss the context in light of the popularity of WWJD.

2. Read a story from the *Martyrs Mirror* or share a story of how Christians are being persecuted today. Has the church in North America lost something?

3. Do you believe Cassie Bernall was a martyr at Columbine High School? Explain.

4. How does economic opportunity clash with our convictions as people of peace?

5. Have someone do a search of kingdom references on a Bible program or look up the word in a concordance. How does this composite picture challenge the popular view of heaven?

6. Are the hard sayings of Jesus out of our reach or should we strive for them this side of heaven?

13

And Who Is Equal to Such a Task?

Anyone can hold the helm when the sea is calm.

—Publilius Syrus[1]

Key Text *2 Corinthians 2:15-16, NIV*

For we are to God the aroma of Christ among those who are being saved and those who are perishing. To the one we are the smell of death; to the other, the fragrance of life. And who is equal to such a task?

"Most preachers do their best preaching when they condemn sins of people who do not attend church," quips Tony Campolo.[2] During the Persian Gulf War in 1991 I was serving as campus pastor at Bluffton College, Bluffton, Ohio. Bluffton has always had a rich mix of students with varied backgrounds and faith traditions. Mennonite students comprise 10 to 20 percent of the student body while the faculty, staff, and board makeup is decidedly Anabaptist in philosophy and commitment. As the Gulf War heated up, there were forum discussions on the war and what it means to be Christian and pacifist. Articles in the student newspaper debated the issues of loyalty to God and country in the context of a historic peace church college. We had a handful of students whose parents or siblings were in the National Guard and sent to the Gulf. Articulating a strong Christian biblical peace position needed to be done with those students in mind. How were they hearing the debate? What did it mean to question the motives of the military when their family members' lives were at risk? While I was giving counsel to one student who was filing a conscientious objector claim seeking release from the National Guard, other students were hurt that the college wasn't more sensitive to their personal and family situation.

What I came to appreciate was that deeply held positions and biblical truths need to be tempered and tested by lived experience. We have to literally *face* the music that not all Christians will agree with our peace stance.

Years later in my first pastorate I came preaching and teaching peace. The church knew of my involvement with MCC Peace Section in the early 1980s and my interest in peace theology. This was a well-established congregation with a long and storied history in the General Conference. They were "conference-minded" and supported missions and peace in practical and tangible ways. When one of our high school seniors got appointed to the Air Force Academy it sparked a series of discussions and debates in Spiritual Council and Sunday school classes. How should we relate to this young man who was baptized and joined the church just a year before? His interest was in becoming a pilot, not killing. Was this a test of membership? In our tradition as a church and denomination (General Conference) it was not. Our teaching and preaching position remained clear but we would continue to relate to this member as we would other college students. "And besides," said one our deacons, "there are other veterans in the church."

That led to the discovery that there were in fact twenty-one veterans in our fellowship. We hosted a series of breakfasts to hear their stories and talk about our understandings of faith and practice.[3] Together we affirmed that the biblical peace position is the teaching of the Mennonite Church as articulated in the *Confession of Faith in a Mennonite Perspective* (Article 22), that this was the teaching position of our church since we had recently adopted the *Confession* as our doctrinal statement, and finally, that those who disagree with this position agree not to teach against it. For me as pastor, it diffused much of the perceived or real tension in the congregation. After preaching a peace sermon one Sunday I received a lengthy letter from a member concerned about how all the veterans might feel about what I had said. Because of the breakfasts I was able to say that "we understand each other." Later, I was called upon to help think and pray through the issue with neighboring Mennonite congregations who did make the peace position a test of membership and now faced situations among their membership that put that teaching to the test. A special gathering was called and I was invited to give the input on Christ's way of peace. That paper became the catalyst for this book. When personal stories, family ties, and Christian relationships are involved, the call of "Agreeing and Disagreeing in Love"[4] is truly put to the test.

Challenging the dominant culture on matters of war, revenge, and the use of violent force is best approached by people of faith in a *confessional* way. During a winter Bible study series at a large Mennonite congregation, one of the members said, "I'm not there yet." He commutes to center city Philadelphia every day and was honest enough to say that he wasn't sure how he would respond if he was attacked leaving work someday. I realized that most of us approach the peace position largely untested. We can't say for *certain* how we would act in a given situation or circumstance. There hasn't been a military call-up (draft) in the United States since 1975 at the tail end of the Vietnam War. Eighteen-year-old males still need to register with the Selective Service System, and the denomination has excellent materials to help them think through their beliefs.[5] But ultimately, we don't know how things will unfold if faced with a situation that threatens our personal safety or challenges our beliefs in nonviolence. Do actions follow beliefs, or do beliefs grow out of our actions? Perhaps some of both. As the illustrations demonstrate, our beliefs need to be tested under the pressure of lived experience. But we dare not wait until we are tested to know what we believe. If we are trained in the ways of peace we are more likely, with God's help, to hold to those beliefs when put to the test.

And who is equal to such a task? Paul approaches the calling of being an apostle with such a confessional approach. He calls us to become "living letters" for Christ. Paul had no credentials, unlike some who peddled their religion for a profit. Paul's only references were his words and actions. He was no salvation salesman trying to hawk a product to whoever would buy. His life and ministry spoke louder than his words and he calls us to do the same.

> For we are not peddlers of God's word like so many; but in Christ we speak as persons of sincerity, as persons sent from God and standing in his presence (2 Cor. 2:17).

Like Paul, we do not minister or give witness to our beliefs on our own power. In the name of Christ and by the power of the Holy Spirit we witness to the way of peace in the world. In the next chapter Paul makes this clear.

> You yourselves are our letter, written on our hearts, to be known and read by all; and you show that you are a letter of Christ, prepared by us, written not with ink but with the Spirit of the living God, not on tablets of stone but on tablets of human hearts (2 Cor 3:2-3).

The challenge for us as Christians and as communities of faith is to continually find ways to allow the Holy Spirit to write on our hearts the message of nonviolence and peace. Bible study, prayer, spiritual discernment, and ultimately testing those beliefs through lived experience opens our hearts, minds, and lives to God's way of love. Once written on our hearts by the Holy Spirit it cannot be erased by the winds of war or cultural challenge. It may divide family and church communities. It may cause us to widen or narrow the circle of church membership. It may tempt us to run away and ignore the hard sayings of Jesus. And who is equal to such a task?

Barry Gorman, men's soccer coach at Penn State University, once said in a coaches' clinic that he never worries too much about his win-loss record. Gorman grew up in Belfast, Northern Ireland, and when he came to the United States and began coaching high school soccer, the school and fans were so obsessed with his win-loss record. He wasn't. Why? "What matters," said Coach Gorman, "is whether your players go on to play at the next level. Are your players trying out for travel team, select team, and Olympic Development? Are they going on to play college soccer? Are they becoming youth coaches and giving something back to the game? That's how you measure success as a coach."[6] So, we get baptized and join the church. Are we playing at the next level of discipleship? Are we giving something back to the Christian faith and community? Are we putting feet to our faith in voluntary service, mission work, and as delegates to conference? Are we using our Spirit-gifts as Sunday school teachers, Bible school helpers, worship leaders, and small-group members? Are we living letters for Christ's way of peace? Are we challenging the dominant cultural assumption of self-preservation at all costs and witnessing to Christ's third way of active nonviolence? And who is equal to such a task?

On our own we will have doubts and times of serious questioning of our beliefs about peace and nonviolence. Sometimes our passions are so strong in the face of injustice or wrongdoing that we wonder if we really are persons of peace or not. "The goal in life is not the quieting of powerful passions—a Greek idea—but the proper use of them—a biblical idea."[7] I once heard the singer Bruce Cockburn in concert during seminary days. His popular song at the time was "If I Had a Rocket Launcher." It reflected his experience in Central America and the terrible violence happening in El Salvador and Guatemala. Helicopter gunships would fly over conflictive zones and often slaughter refugees who were fleeing their contested villages and farms. Cockburn sings, "If I had a rocket launcher, I'd make somebody pay." Loyal fans were dismayed and critics pointed to the inconsistency of his words and his professed Christian faith. In concert, however, he took extra time to introduce this particular song. He said that as a musician he had to find a constructive way to deal with his deep feelings and frustrations in the face of injustice. Singing this song every night in performance was his way of working out those passions. He said he would never act on them, but they needed to be dealt with.[8] That was an important lesson for me to hear. The feelings themselves are not the problem. What we do with them is. Sometimes I lash out at my children for being insubordinate or petty. And when I do I feel terrible. I've become exactly what I was most upset at them about! Thankfully, the majority of the time I'm able to take a deep breath, pray myself through it, and not do anything I will regret later. As peacemakers we must guard against fundamentalism. We are too often intolerant of those who do not share our convictions. We are quick to cut off, condemn, and counter those who have chosen a different path. Grace and a reminder that it is God who does the changing of a person's heart, not us, allows us to approach our Christian peacemaking in a confessional way.

And who is equal to such a task? On our own, no one. But with God's help and the guidance of the Holy Spirit and in the context of Christian community, we can challenge the assumption of self-preservation and give witness to Christ's way of peace. May it be so for us.

Questions for Discussion

1. Can you give other examples of how easy it is to condemn sinful behavior when the sinners aren't in our midst?
2. How have you or members of your group dealt with controversial issues when they involved members of your church?
3. Is nonviolence a test of membership in your church? Was it in the past? Should it be?
4. Do you agree with the assertion that thinking through

potential situations of violence with nonviolent solutions helps us prepare for an alternative response. Give examples.

5. Think of ways you or your group can take your faith "to the next level" of discipleship. How can you be a "living letter for Christ" regarding Christian peacemaking?

Notes

Chapter 1

1. Character line in *The X-Files* movie/video, Twentieth Century Fox, 1998.

2. Albert N. Keim, *Harold S. Bender 1897-1962* (Scottdale: Herald Press, 1998). As serialized in *Mennonite Weekly Review* (Jan. 25, 2001), 13.

3. In class I use a summary of *What Would You Do?* by John Howard Yoder, (Scottdale: Herald Press, 1983).

4. Julia Esquival, *Threatened with Resurrection. Prayers and Poems from an Exiled Guatemalan* (Elgin, Ill.: Brethren Press, 1982), 59. I'm indebted to this book which first introduced me to the idea of being *threatened with resurrection*. A working vacation to Central America over Christmas 1983 to New Years 1984 forced me to wrestle with issues of faith and mortality in new ways. Esquival's poetry and faith gave voice to those learnings.

Chapter 2

1. Rodney A. Clapp, *A Peculiar People* (Downers Grove: InterVarsity Press, 1996), 82.

2. Robert S. Krieder, "Let a Hundred Flowers Bloom" and "One Lord, One Faith, One Baptism," *Mennonite Quarterly Review* 53:3 (July 1983): 186. Kreider describes growing up in Bluffton, Ohio, in the 1930s and recalls when three Russian Mennonite families moved to town, including my grandparents.

3. Richard B. Gardner, Elmer A. Martens, and Howard H. Charles editors, Believers Church Bible Commentary: *Matthew* (Scottdale: Herald Press), 258.

4. As quoted in Harry Loewen and Steven Nolt, *Through Fire and Water: An Overview of Mennonite History* (Scottdale: Herald Press, 1996), 15.

5. *Interpreter's Dictionary of the Bible, Vol. 3* (Nashville: Abingdon Press), 288.

Chapter 3

1. The source of the exact wording of this quote eludes me (given to me as a gift) but the sentiment is expressed in Barclay's *Daily Study Bible Series* on 1 Peter 1:1-2, rev. ed. (Philadelphia: Westminster, 1996), 168. *We must repeat that this does not mean withdrawal from the world; but it does mean that the Christian sees all things in the light of eternity and life as a journey toward God. It is this which decides the importance which he attaches to anything; it is this which dictates his conduct. It is the touchstone and the dynamics of his life.*

2. Thieleman J. van Braght, *The Bloody Theater or Martyrs Mirror of the Defenseless Christians.* 12th ed. (Scottdale: Herald Press, 1979).

3. William E. Moore, late captain, USA, and James C. Russell, late captain, USA, *U.S. Official Pictures of the World War: Showing America's Participation. Selected from the Official Files of the War Department* (Washington, D.C.: Pictorial Bureau, 1928), 3.

4. *Interpreter's Dictionary of the Bible, Vol. 1* (Nashville: Abingdon, 1962), 749.

5. Joyce M. Shutt as printed in *The Mennonite* 93:39 (Oct. 31, 1978): 638.

6. I first learned of the inverted triangle through an e-mail preaching discussion group (Preaching the Revised Common Lectionary, Nov. 22, 1995, post from Don Genge, Peterborough, Ont.). The social hierarchy of Jesus' day is well documented in Joachim Jeremias, *Jerusalem in the Time of Jesus: An Investigation into the Economic and Social Conditions During the New Testament Period* (Philadelphia: Fortress, 1969). Also Eduard Lohse, *The New Testament Environment,* translated by John E. Steely (Nashville: Abingdon, 1971).

7. Donald Kraybill, *The Upside-Down Kingdom* (Scottdale: Herald Press, 1978). A must-read for every generation of radical Christians.

Chapter 4

1. Morton Kelsey, *Spiritual Living in a Material World: A Practical Guide* (New York: New City Press, 1998), 55.

2. Sandra M. Schneiders, "Death in the Community of Eternal Life: History, Theology, and Spirituality in John 11," as appeared in *Interpretation* 41:1 (Jan. 1987).

3. Kelsey, *Spiritual Living,* 55.

Chapter 5

1. John Driver, *Community and Commitment* (Scottdale: Herald Press, 1976), 28.

2. John Howard Yoder, *What Would You Do?* (Scottdale: Herald Press, 1983), 20.

3. Ibid., 18.

4. *Confession of Faith in a Mennonite Perspective*, Article 22, "Peace, Justice, and Nonresistance" (Scottdale: Herald Press, 1995), 82.

5. For an excellent visual portrayal of Anabaptist martyrdom see *The Radicals* (Gateway Films: Vision Video, © 1989, Sisters and Brothers).

6. Rachelle Schlabach, "U.S. Aid Fuels War, Colombian Says," *Mennonite Weekly Review* (Nov. 9, 2000): 1.

7. Melanie Zuercher, "Colombia Worker Lives in 'Resurrection Hope,'" *Mennonite Weekly Review* (Nov. 16, 2000): 9.

Chapter 6

1. Robert Van De Weyer, *Celtic Prayers: A Book of Celtic Devotion. Daily Prayers and Blessings,* (Nashville: Abingdon Press, 1997), 26.

2. See Mother Teresa's website at www.catholic.net/RCC/people/mother/teresa/teresa.html. The introductory page reflects that "Mother would see Jesus in everyone that she met."

3. Bernhard Anderson, *Out of the Depths: The Psalms Speak for Us Today* (Louisville: Westminster John Knox, 1974), 148.

4. Pearl S. Buck, "The Missionary's Wife in China," in A. Ruth Fry ed., *Victories Without Violence* (London: Denis Dobson, 1939), 69-71.

5. For more on Christian hospitality see Michelle Hershberger, *A Christian View of Hospitality: Expecting Surprises* (Scottdale: Herald Press, 1999).

Chapter 7

1. As quoted in *The Balkans: Wounded and Searching for Peace*, a Mennonite Central Committee video.

2. "Would You Kill Idi Amin?" *Campus Life* (December, 1977): 57. The thirteen leaders who answered the question are Charles Colson, Ann Kiemel, Pat Boone, Tom Skinner, Harold Myra, John Powell, S.J., Catherine Marshall LeSourd, Kefa Sempangi, Marabel Morgan, Anita Bryant, Festo Kivengere, Rev. Michael Wurmbrand, and Jay Kesler.

3. Ibid, 84.

4. Ibid. Kefa Sempangi witnessed to the secret policeman assigned to kill him and won him to Christ. The same man later helped Sempangi escape Uganda. Festo Kivengere authored the book *I Love Idi Amin* while in exile.

5. Jim Amstutz, *Samaritans in the Gospels*, unpublished paper, (Nov. 30, 1984).

6. Wilma Bailey has written an important corrective on why the "Good" Samaritan isn't. "How do we figure out what we are supposed to do: Not good, just a Samaritan," *Gospel Herald* 87:33 (August 23, 1994): 6-7. Nowhere in the text does Jesus call the Samaritan good. Samaritan ethics and religious practice required any lay person to assist another in need, even an enemy.

Chapter 8

1. "A Mighty Fortress Is Our God," v. 4, based on Psalm 46, as published in *The Mennonite Hymnal* (Scottdale: Herald Press, 1969), no. 325.

2. Yoder, *What Would You Do?*, 39.

3. John K. Stoner and Lois Barrett, *Letters to American Christians* (Scottdale: Herald Press, 1989), 23-4. (Out of print but available from New Call to Peacemaking, P.O. Box 500, Akron, PA 17501.)

4. See Susan Classen, *Vultures and Butterflies: Living the Contradictions* (Scottdale: Herald Press, 1992). Susan was one of the nurses assigned to the conflictive zone in El Salvador and was eventually detained and questioned by the authorities.

5. *I Pledge Allegiance to the Lamb* by Ray Boltz. Word Music, Inc. and Shepherd Boy Music, 1994. Used by permission.

Chapter 9

1. *Confession of Faith in a Mennonite Perspective*, Article 24 "The Reign of God," (Scottdale: Herald Press, 1995), 89.

2. Mirislov Volf, *Exclusion and Embrace: A Theological Exploration of Identity, Otherness, and Reconciliation* (Nashville: Abingdon, 1996), 298. Here

Volf points to Walter Klaassen, *Anabaptism in Outline* (Scottdale: Herald Press, 1981), 316-44.

3. *Confession of Faith*, 91.

4. Yoder, *What Would You Do?*, 40.

5. For a dramatic portrayal of the early Anabaptist struggle with church-state issues see *The Radicals*, op. cit.

6. Volf, *Exclusion and Embrace*, 302.

7. See Article 22 "Peace, Justice, and Nonresistance" in *Confession of Faith in a Mennonite Perspective*.

8. Christopher Marshall, "Following Christ Down Under: A New Zealand Perspective on Anabaptism," in John D. Roth, ed., *Engaging Anabaptism: Conversations with a Radical Tradition* (Scottdale: Herald Press, 2001), for a provocative discussion of how the nonviolence of Jesus reflects the essential nature of God and thus warrants a search for a non-retributive or nonviolent way of understanding hell and final judgment while remaining true to the scriptures.

Chapter 10

1. Helen Keller, "Strike Against War," speech delivered before the Women's Peace Party at New York, N.Y. (January 5, 1916). Text taken from American Foundation for the Blind, www.afb.org/archives/intro.html.

2. Vernard Eller, *King Jesus' Manual of Arms for the Armless: War and Peace from Genesis to Revelation* (Nashville: Abingdon, 1973), 176.

3. Richard McSorely, "The Gospel of Peace," *The Mennonite* 96:29 (August 11, 1981): 455.

4. Ibid.

5. Eller, *King Jesus' Manual*, 144.

6. John Stott, *Romans: God's Good News for the World* (Downers Grove, Ill.: InterVarsity Press, 1994), 337.

Chapter 11

1. Walter Wink, *Engaging the Powers* (Minneapolis: Fortress Press, 1992), 175. Much of this chapter is indebted to Wink's work in chapter 9 of *Engaging the Powers*.

2. As quoted by the Mahatma Gandhi Foundation at www.mahatma.org (http://web.mahatma.org.in/test/quotes.text).

3. Millar Burrows, *The Dead Sea Scrolls* (New York: Viking Press, 1955), 380.

4. Philip Blackman, *Mishnayoth, Vol. IV, Order Nezikin* (New York, Judaica Press, 1963), 66.

5. As quoted in Walter Wink, *Violence and Nonviolence in South Africa: Jesus' Third Way* (Philadelphia: New Society Publishers, 1987), 19.

6. *The Works of Flavius Josephus*, translated by William Whiston (Hartford: S.S. Scranton Co., 1902), 551.

7. Christian Peacemaker Teams, P.O. Box 6508, Chicago, IL 60680, e-mail cpt@igc.org, web www.prairienet.org/cpt.

Chapter 12

1. Character in *My Dog Skip*, Warner Studios, July 11, 2000. Based on the book by Willie Morris. Jenkins was the local high school sports hero drafted into combat during WWII. He came home in disgrace as a deserter.

2. Charles M. Sheldon, *In His Steps* (Carmel, N.Y.: Guideposts Associates, 1962). The book cover claims "*In His Steps* is the most popular book ever written, except the Bible."

3. Available for $20.00 from Mennonite Board of Missions, Box 370, Elkhart, IN 46515-0370.

4. Misty Bernell, *She Said Yes: The Unlikely Martyrdom of Cassie Bernall* (Farmington, Pa.: Plough Publishing House, 1999).

5. Diana Butler Bass, "'Cassie' Book and the Hellfire Hype," *Chicago Tribune* (October 6, 1999): Commentary, 21.

6. Ibid.

7. Pastor Melvin Schmidt at the funeral of Bonnie Kehler at First Mennonite Church, Bluffton, Ohio, January 5, 1986.

8. Rodney Stark, *The Rise of Christianity* (San Francisco: Harper Collins, 1996), 167.

9. The town of Virgin, Utah, enacted an ordinance requiring a gun and ammunition in every home for residents' self-defense. The mentally ill, convicted felons, conscientious objectors, and people who cannot afford to own a gun are exempt. Associated Press story, *The Morning Call*, Allentown, Pa. (Monday, November 6, 2000): A2.

10. Kraybill, *Upside-Down Kingdom*, 10.

11. William Barclay, *The Lord's Prayer* (Louisville: Westminster John Knox Press, 1998), 74.

Chapter 13

1. James Hewitt, ed., *Illustrations Unlimited* (Wheaton: Tyndale, 1988), 132.

2. Tony Campolo, *Is Jesus a Republican or a Democrat? And 14 Other Polarizing Issues* (Waco: Word Books, 1995), 19.

3. See Jim Amstutz, "Eating breakfast with Mennonite soldiers," *Gospel Herald* 90:34 (January 2, 1997): 6-7.

4. Denominational statement and process for Mennonites in times of disagreement adopted by the joint Mennonite Assembly, Wichita, Kan., July 1995. See also Katie Day, *Difficult Conversations: Taking Risks, Acting with Integrity* (Bethesda, Md.: The Alban Institute, 2001).

5. *Decide for Peace* is available from the Mennonite Church USA offices, 722 Main St., Box 347, Newton, KS 67114-0347.

6. Barry Gorman, guest speaker at the Ephrata, Pa. Youth Soccer Association coaches clinic, March 20, 1993.

7. Sean Caulfield, *Under the Broom Tree* (Mahwah, New Jersey: Paulist Press, 1982), 24.

8. Bruce Cockburn, "If I Had a Rocket Launcher," Stealing Fire, 1984. In 1984 Cockburn wrote, "In fact, I almost didn't put 'Rocket Launcher' on the album because of the ease with which it could be misinterpreted." For additional comments see cockburnproject.net/songs&music/iiharl.html.

Select Bibliography

Augsburger, Myron S. *The Robe of God: Reconciliation, the Believers Church Essential.* Scottdale: Herald Press, 2000.

Bernall, Misty. *She Said Yes: The Unlikely Martyrdom of Cassie Bernall.* Farmington, Pa.: Plough Publishing House, 1999.

Classen, Susan. *Vultures and Butterflies: Living the Contradictions.* Scottdale: Herald Press, 1992.

Clapp, Rodney A. *A Peculiar People.* Downers Grove, Ill.: InterVarsity Press, 1996.

Confession of Faith in a Mennonite Perspective. Scottdale: Herald Press, 1995.

Day, Katie. *Difficult Conversations: Taking Risks, Acting with Integrity.* Bethesda, Md.: The Alban Institute, 2001.

Driedger, Leo and Donald B. Kraybill. *Mennonite Peacemaking: From Quietism to Activism.* Scottdale: Herald Press, 1994.

Eller, Vernard. *War and Peace from Genesis to Revelation.* Nashville: Abingdon, 1973.

Esquival, Julia. *Threatened with Resurrection: Prayers and Poems from an Exiled Guatemalan.* Elgin, Ill.: Brethren Press, 1982.

Friesen, Duane K. *Christian Peacemaking & International Conflict: A Realist Pacifist Perspective.* Scottdale: Herald Press, 1986.

Herr, Robert and Judy Zimmerman Herr, eds. *Transforming Violence: Linking Local and Global Peacemaking.* Scottdale: Herald Press, 1998.

Hershberger, Michelle. *A Christian View of Hospitality: Expecting Surprises.* Scottdale: Herald Press, 1999.

Kelsey, Morton. *Spiritual Living in a Material World: A Practical Guide.* New York: New City Press, 1998.

Kraybill, Donald. *The Upside-Down Kingdom.* Scottdale: Herald Press, 1978.

Lederach, John Paul. *The Journey Toward Reconciliation.* Scottdale: Herald Press, 1999.

Mitton, Michael. *The Soul of Celtic Spirituality: In the Lives of Its Saints.* Mystic: Twenty-Third Publications, 1996.

Stark, Rodney. *The Rise of Christianity.* San Francisco: HarperCollins, 1997.

Volf, Mirislov. *Exclusion and Embrace: A Theological Exploration of Identity, Otherness, and Reconciliation.* Nashville: Abingdon, 1996.

Wink, Walter. *Engaging the Powers.* Minneapolis: Fortress Press, 1992.

Yoder, John Howard. *The Politics of Jesus.* Grand Rapids: Eerdmans, 1972.

_____*What Would You Do?* Scottdale: Herald Press, 1983.

Scripture Index

The Author

Christi Delp

Jim S. Amstutz has been involved in peace work for the last twenty-five years. During the early 1980s he was the director of Draft Counselor Training and Peace Education for Mennonite Central Committee (MCC) U.S. Peace Section. In that role he traveled extensively in the United States conducting peace and draft counseling workshops. Jim is currently the pastor of Akron Mennonite Church in Akron, Pennsylvania. He and his wife, Lorraine, are parents of three children.